Betrayal & Beyond

JOURNAL

FASHIONING A COURAGEOUS HEART
Diane Roberts and Shari Chinchen

BETRAYAL & BEYOND JOURNAL

By Diane Roberts and Shari Chinchen

Other contributing writers:
Ted Roberts
Jane Carter
Teri Vietti
Elizabeth Drago

Copyright © 2016 by Ted & Diane Roberts

Published by
Pure Desire Ministries International
719 NE Roberts Avenue, Gresham, OR 97030
www.puredesire.org | 503.489.0230
ISBN 978-1-943291-10-6

The stories presented of individual lives in this *Journal* are true and accurate. The details have been adjusted to prevent personal identification. In some cases the story presented is a compilation of the histories of several individuals. The compilation, however, doesn't affect the clinical or theological veracity of the stories.

TABLE OF CONTENTS

MANAGING THE CRISIS

The journey toward healing from betrayal is not an easy one. It requires us to leave behind our status quo, to face the challenge before us, to accept support from others who understand this challenge, and to strive toward the beauty that lies beyond. This journey requires courage; it requires you to embrace your own *hero's journey*. Our prayer is that you will boldly choose this journey as you walk through *Betrayal & Beyond*.

Journaling can be a powerful tool in this healing process. One woman reported, "My heart, my entire body was filled with so much hurt, anger, and emotions, I couldn't begin to speak out what I was feeling. But as I began to journal, it felt like all the emotions I had been carrying around were released. It was as if they were traveling out of my heart, through my veins, through the pen and onto the paper. God began healing me as I expressed and released what was in my heart." We have included the Feelings Wheel in the *Workbook* appendix, page 291 to help you better identify what you might be feeling as you walk through this *Journal*.

Proverbs cautions:

> *Above all else, guard your heart, for everything you do flows from it.*
> PROVERBS 4:23 (NIV)

The only way we can guard our heart is to discover and release what is in our heart.

As you fill this *Journal*, God can give you a new perspective and clarity as He speaks His *rhema* word to you. That *rhema* word is a personal word from God that can carry you through each day, helping you continue on your *hero's journey*.

You may be thinking, "What do you mean by a *hero's journey*? What does it have to do with me?" Very good questions!

The *hero's journey* or, perhaps more appropriately for us, the *heroine's journey*, describes the classic story pattern which can be boiled down to three stages:

STAGE ONE

The *departure* from the *ordinary life* or *status quo*, as the *heroine* receives her *call to action*, may attempt to *refuse the call*, and meets *the mentor* who will help her along her journey.

EXAMPLE
Consider the story of Esther:

Her *ordinary life/status quo* was disrupted by her *call to action* when she was taken to the palace to marry the king (Esther 2:8). Her cousin and Mentor, Mordecai, advises her not to reveal that she is a Jewess, and continues to mentor her at the palace.

STAGE TWO

The *initiation*, where the *heroine* begins her *quest* and is confronted by ever increasing *obstacles* and *challenges* that she must overcome.

EXAMPLE
At Haman's instigation, the king issues an edict to exterminate all Jews. Mordecai sends word to Esther that she must go to the king and stop the decree from becoming reality and, thus, begin her *quest*. Esther is afraid to approach the king without permission, as that would be a death sentence. Mordecai convinces Esther that she has been placed in her royal position for such a time as this (Esther 4:14). Esther asks her people to fast and pray for three days, courageously resolves "If I die, I die," and then goes to see the king (Esther 4:16). She invites the king and Haman to a series of feasts; during the final feast, she reveals her identity as a Jewess and states that Haman is trying to kill her and her people. The king is outraged, and has Haman hanged. She has overcome her *obstacles* and *challenges*.

STAGE THREE

The return, as the *heroine* claims her *reward*, emerges from the battle with new strength and new skills, and begins an upgraded *status quo*.

EXAMPLE
The king realizes the damage Haman has caused and appoints Mordecai as his new Prime Minister. Mordecai and Esther issue their first edict which grants Jews the right to defend themselves against harm. Esther's heroic choice to accept her *call to action* and face her *challenge* not only saves her and Mordecai from certain death, but also saves her entire nation from destruction. Esther has claimed her *reward*, has emerged from her battle with new strength, and settles into a new and upgraded *status quo*.

By stepping into this process, you are embarking on your own *heroine's journey*. You have been called out of your *status quo*, not by your own choosing, but because of your husband's addiction. This is your *call to action* for this season of your life. You may prefer to refuse that call, but you have met other women in your Betrayal & Beyond group who can mentor you through this journey. You will face *obstacles* and *challenges* along the way, but as you immerse yourself in your *Workbook* and *Journal*, you will learn new skills and develop strength you never knew you had. As you succeed over that which the enemy has used to attempt to destroy you and your marriage, perhaps you, like Esther, will be raised up to help others for such a time as this. This will be your *reward*.

This is a journey that requires great courage. Yes, there will be times you will experience fear, but your fellow heroines will be there to buoy you up and keep you from continuing in a journey of fear. The section below can help contrast the difference between a courageous journey and a fearful one.

CHAPTER ONE

A COURAGEOUS JOURNEY
I am courageous enough to share my journey with others. I will risk my story with others who can help me through this process.

A FEARFUL JOURNEY
I will remain stuck in isolation and shame. I will not allow others to see my pain, or help me through this time.

SCRIPTURAL REFERENCE

Therefore confess your sins to each other and pray for each other so that you may be healed. The prayer of a righteous person is powerful and effective.
JAMES 5:16 (NIV)

CHAPTER TWO

A COURAGEOUS JOURNEY
I am willing to understand that sex addiction is both a moral and a brain problem.

A FEARFUL JOURNEY
I refuse to accept new information that may help me gain a new insight.

SCRIPTURAL REFERENCE

'Call to Me, and I will answer you,
and show you great and mighty things, which you do not know.'
JEREMIAH 33:3 (NKJV)

Do not conform to the pattern of this world,
but be transformed by the renewing of your mind.
ROMANS 12:2A (NIV)

CHAPTER THREE

A COURAGEOUS JOURNEY
I will trust that God is bigger than whatever I face.

I will hold in tension the reality of what I am facing with the hope of what God is speaking to me about my future.

A FEARFUL JOURNEY
I allow the enemy to intimidate me with overwhelming fear.

I put a wall around my pain, stuff it inside me, and believe that the enemy will destroy everything. I have no hope.

SCRIPTURAL REFERENCE

Now to Him who is able to do immeasurably more than all we ask or imagine,
according to His power that is at work within us,
EPHESIANS 3:20 (NIV)

*"For I know the plans I have for you," says the L*ORD*, "plans to prosper you and not*
to harm you, plans to give you hope and a future."
JEREMIAH 29:11 (NIV)

be careful w/ this verse! God is speaking to the Israelites.

CHAPTER FOUR

A COURAGEOUS JOURNEY
I am willing to face my own pain and shame.

A FEARFUL JOURNEY
I try to please everyone, and I don't establish healthy boundaries.

SCRIPTURAL REFERENCE

...looking unto Jesus, the author and finisher of our faith, who for the joy that was set before Him endured the cross, despising the shame, and has sat down at the right hand of the throne of God.
HEBREWS 12:2 (NKJV)

CHAPTER FIVE

A COURAGEOUS JOURNEY
I am able to discern between a burden and a load, and I can appropriately help others. I practice good self-care.

A FEARFUL JOURNEY
I take others' burdens upon myself, often times ignoring my own needs. I rescue others from the negative consequences of their own choices.

SCRIPTURAL REFERENCE

Carry each other's burdens...[but]... each one should carry their own load.
GALATIANS 6:2A,5 (NIV)

CHAPTER SIX

A COURAGEOUS JOURNEY
I allow natural consequences to play out. I do not rescue others from their poor choices.

A FEARFUL JOURNEY
I rescue others from their own poor choices.

SCRIPTURAL REFERENCE

Do not be deceived, God is not mocked; for whatever a man sows, that he will also reap.
GALATIANS 6:7 (NKJV)

CHAPTER SEVEN

A COURAGEOUS JOURNEY
I am in touch with my own feelings, including anger, loss, and betrayal. I am able to manage my emotions appropriately.

A FEARFUL JOURNEY
I ignore my own feelings and needs as I placate others' feelings and needs, and allow my anger to control me.

SCRIPTURAL REFERENCE

My heart is in anguish within me; the terrors of death have fallen on me. Fear and trembling have beset me; horror has overwhelmed me.
PSALM 55:4-5 (NIV)

"In your anger do not sin": Do not let the sun go down while you are still angry,
EPHESIANS 4:26 (NIV)

CHAPTER EIGHT

A COURAGEOUS JOURNEY
I understand the difference between forgiveness and reconciliation, and can choose to forgive.

A FEARFUL JOURNEY
I am unable to forgive and I continue to walk in unforgiveness and shaming.

Or

I prematurely forgive others' poor behavior.

SCRIPTURAL REFERENCE

And forgive us our debts, as we also have forgiven our debtors.
MATTHEW 6:12 (NIV)

"The king summoned the man and said, 'You evil servant! I forgave your entire debt when you begged me for mercy. Shouldn't you be compelled to be merciful to your fellow servant who asked for mercy?'"
MATTHEW 18:32-33 (MSG)

3. TRUSTING OTHERS

Therefore confess your sins to each other and pray for each other so that you may be healed. The prayer of a righteous person is powerful and effective.
[In this case, confess your needs to one another.]
JAMES 5:16 (NIV)

_____

_____

_____

_____

_____

_____

4. GETTING IN TOUCH WITH YOUR OWN FEELINGS AND NEEDS

David's response to Betrayal by Saul:

❓ **How can you relate to these feelings?**

My heart is in anguish within me; the terrors of death have fallen on me.
Fear and trembling have beset me; horror has overwhelmed me.
[Lord, save me!]
PSALM 55:4-5 (NIV)

_____

_____

_____

_____

_____

_____

⊙ If you completed a collage during your orientation, describe what you learned about yourself and your situation as you described your collage to the group.

_____

_____

_____

_____

ROAD SIGNS FOR YOUR JOURNEY

Your _Journal_ contains some or all of the following elements for each week's lesson:

Going Deeper by exploring and processing material in the _Betrayal & Beyond Workbook_.

Meditating on God's Word and allowing Him to speak into my situation.

Telling My Story through identifying and processing my pain, I can approach life with a healthy perspective. I will no longer need to react to pain from the past.

A (Courageous) Challenge for the Week: What fears am I boldly facing, or commitments am I surrendering to this week that will move me out of my comfort zone and challenge me to risk?

The Commitment to Change addresses a challenge you will be facing during the week.

The FASTER Scale is a tool for healing through understanding your addictive behaviors.

The Group Check-in allows you to log your progress and commitments.

Journal the fears or emotions you might be feeling about sharing your story with your group. Most women have never shared their story, so this will be a new area for you to learn to risk and trust others.

_____

_____

_____

_____

_____

_____

_____

_____

_____

What am I trusting God for today, especially in light of finishing week 2 of journaling.

_____

_____

_____

_____

_____

_____

_____

_____

_____

_____

After sharing your story with the women in your group, how might Henri Nouwen's statement be true in your life?

Henri Nouwen eloquently states the benefits of healing in community:

> Healing begins not where our pain is taken away, but where it can be shared and seen as part of a larger pain. The first task of healing, therefore, is to take our many problems and pains out of their isolation and place them at the center of the great battle against the Evil One....As we create the space to mourn—whether through one-to-one relationships, small groups, or communal celebrations—we free ourselves little by little from the grip of the Evil One and come to discover in the midst of our grief that the same Spirit who calls us to mourn stirs us to make the first movement in our dance with God...[1]

1. Henri J.M. Nouwen, *The Only Necessary Thing* (New York: The Crossroad Publishing Company, 1999) 151.

Lesson Four

WHAT DO I DO NOW?
WHERE DO I GO FROM HERE?

Thought for the week: *This is the week you truly begin your quest. As you move forward, remember that God is bigger than whatever you face.*

Journal about your feelings after reading His Reality, Her Reality.

_____

_____

_____

_____

_____

_____

Journal some of your feelings about the emotional baggage that has been dumped on you because of his sexual activity.

_____

_____

_____

_____

_____

_____

_____

How might this Scripture bring you comfort?

Carry each other's burdens, and in this way you will fulfill the law of Christ.

GALATIANS 6:2 (NIV)

_____

_____

_____

_____

_____

_____

_____

_____

_____

What are your reactions to the information about premature forgiveness in this lesson? Journal your thoughts:

_____

_____

_____

_____

_____

_____

_____

_____

JOURNAL YOUR DECLARATION OF AUTHORITY OVER THESE AREAS:

Identify some things that you know you need to take authority with respect to your husband's addiction (e.g. spirit of lust, denial, behaviors counter to Christ-likeness, anger, childhood wounds).

_____

_____

_____

_____

_____

_____

_____

_____

What are some things you need to speak over your home and your children for safety and protection (e.g. a spirit of peace, health, protection from any spirits of which your husband is involved)?

_____

_____

_____

_____

_____

_____

_____

_____

_____

In light of the Scriptures shared in your lesson this week and what you have learned so far, write out a prayer for your husband.

You may still be struggling emotionally because of the hurt and betrayal, and that is normal. But we are called to walk where Jesus did; while He was on the cross, He was praying for those who had betrayed and crucified Him. Ask Him to help you write a prayer, one that He would pray for your husband.

_____

_____

_____

_____

_____

_____

_____

_____

_____

_____

_____

_____

_____

_____

_____

_____

_____

_____

_____

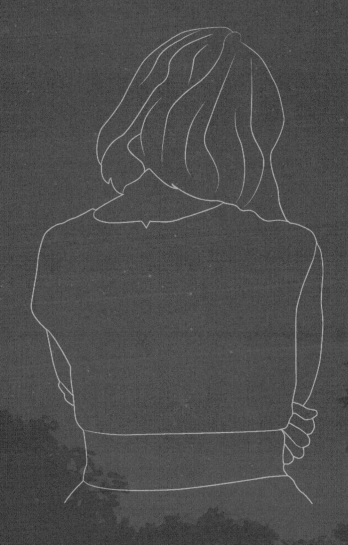

Chapter Two

UNDERSTANDING THE NATURE OF ADDICTION

ⓓ Lesson One
UNDERSTANDING ADDICTION AND HEALING

Thought for the week: As you continue on this journey, you may experience feelings you can't identify, or mood swings that seem uncontrollable. You can use The Feelings Wheel we've included in the Workbook appendix, page 291 to help you identify your feelings. Remember to access your support networks, and to practice self-care during this time. You are important.

In your *Betrayal & Beyond Workbook* you were challenged to do the following:

If you can, ask your husband if he had a deep sense of worthlessness or feelings of inadequacy. You were asked to write down his response. Then journal your observations about his response.

_____

_____

_____

_____

_____

_____

_____

_____

_____

_____

_____

_____

Your view of God is the most important thing in your life. That affects how you see yourself. In your *Workbook* you were asked to answer the following questions:

How do you see yourself? Write down the view you have.

_____

_____

_____

_____

Write down the view you think your husband has of himself.

_____

_____

_____

_____

Do you see yourself as a sinner who struggles to love God or a lover of God who struggles with sin?

_____

_____

_____

_____

Look back over this week's lesson and share why you've come to these conclusions.

_____

_____

_____

Meditate on John 14:6-18. Write the answers to the following questions in light of this Scripture.

How have you seen God's grace at work in your life?

_____

_____

_____

_____

_____

_____

_____

_____

Review the noose of addiction in Chapter 1, Lesson 2. Explain in your own words how a new understanding of grace might help prevent the Acting in and Acting out cycle. (Hint: What drives addiction?)

_____

_____

_____

_____

_____

_____

_____

CHAPTER 2 | LESSON 4 | WEEK 8

In what ways is Jesus seeking to fill you up more and encouraging you to bring a larger bucket rather than a thimble? (Hint: It probably includes risking on your part.)

_____

_____

_____

_____

_____

_____

_____

_____

_____

_____

Write a prayer for your husband to understand the need for a full disclosure, not just for your sake, but also in light of Deuteronomy and the generational curse.

_____

_____

_____

_____

_____

_____

_____

_____

_____

_____

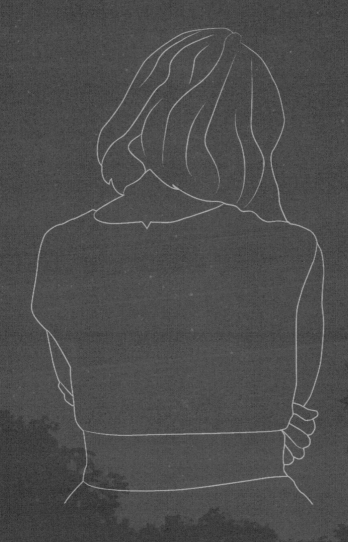

Chapter Three

COMMITMENT TO PERSONAL HEALING

ⓘ *Lesson One*
WHAT IS BROKEN IN OUR MARRIAGE?

Thought for the week: *As you begin to look at your "brokenness," practice compassion for yourself. You are not blaming your family of origin; you are seeking to understand your own reactions.*

Take time to write how you feel concerning those who dropped you.

_____

_____

_____

_____

_____

_____

In light of what was shared about internal brokenness, blind spots, and how our reactions can be limbic because of what has happened in our past, write out how this Scripture in Proverbs might be important in your journey of healing.

> *Above all else, guard your heart, for everything you do flows from it..*
> PROVERBS 4:23 (NIV)

_____

_____

_____

_____

_____

Because of past brokenness and times you have been dropped, identify your vulnerabilities and share wise ways you can respond rather than react.

CRIPPLEDNESS IN MY LIFE

1. Dealing with conflicts and differences in close relationships

_____

_____

_____

_____

_____

_____

2. Dealing with money and budgeting in family relationships

_____

_____

_____

_____

_____

_____

3. Dealing with children and how to discipline them

_____

_____

_____

_____

_____

4. Discussing sexual frustrations and expectations

_____

_____

_____

_____

_____

5. Dealing with personal hurts and wounds in the relationship

_____

_____

_____

_____

_____

Looking at the categories you noticed crippledness in your life, journal some feelings and observations about your struggles.

_____

_____

_____

_____

_____

_____

_____

_____

Most of us had earthly fathers who failed us in some way. Statistics show how important a father's love is to a child's emotional health. Sixty percent of children with low father contact have low self-esteem. Children of both sexes and all ages feel their mothers show more love and affection than their fathers. For children thirteen and under, forty percent of fathers, compared to sixty percent of mothers frequently hug them. Twenty-five percent of fathers and ten percent of mothers hardly ever hug.[3] These statistics are from 20 years ago - so think how detached children must feel today, with the further disintegration of the family.

Where is the hope? In Romans 8:15-17, Scripture says that when we accept Christ as our Savior, we become part of a new bloodline. We have been adopted as daughters and heirs of God. In light of that fact, think about God as our Abba Daddy.

As you look up these verses, describe in your own words who God the Father is in light of Scripture:

DEUTERONOMY 1:31

_____

_____

_____

MATTHEW 6:26, 31-33

_____

_____

_____

MATTHEW 7:11

_____

_____

_____

3. Earl Grollman and Gerri Sweder, _The Working Parent Dilemma: How to Balance the Responsibilities of Children and Careers_ (Beacon Press, Boston, 1986).

PSALM 68:5

_____

_____

_____

From these Scriptures, how is Father God similar/different from your earthly father?

_____

_____

_____

_____

_____

Genesis 1:27 tells us that God created male and female in His image. That means Adam alone does not reflect the totality of the image of God. Therefore, God's parenting of us reflects the qualities of both a mother and father.

In the following Scriptures, explain in your own words how God fulfills the role of a mother.

ISAIAH 66:13

_____

_____

_____

ISAIAH 49:15

_____

_____

_____

LUKE 13:34

_____

_____

_____

If you are a mother or someday hope to be, how would you comfort your child?

_____

_____

_____

_____

_____

Zephaniah 3:17 (1917 JPS) says that God comforts you in this way:

> _The Mighty One will save;_
> _He will rejoice over you with gladness,_
> _He will quiet you with His love,_
> _He will rejoice over you with singing._

Right now, allow God to comfort you by writing out a prayer expressing your needs. Allow yourself to see God rejoicing, singing over you and touching you with His love.

_____

_____

_____

_____

_____

_____

In light of these Scriptures about God the Father, what are some things you wish could have been different in your family of origin? Remember, in order to change patterns, you have to identify what needs to be different.

_____

_____

_____

_____

_____

Now look for patterns that you think God might want to change, not only for you, but also for your children. What would those new patterns look like? (Hint: Look back over the questions 1-30 from the FACES Evaluation and write down the characteristics that were missing in your family of origin that you want to change.)

_____

_____

_____

_____

_____

You have two challenges this week: Identify the patterns you want to change, but also ask God to help you change those patterns. As we yield to the transforming work of the Holy Spirit, this Scripture gives us hope for change for the future.

_____

_____

_____

_____

_____

Journal on your Double Bind related to trusting God. (You may want to write a prayer that reflects the fears you want to release to Him or the action steps that feel uncomfortable.)

If I choose to trust God and surrender to Him (what fears will I have to face?):

_____

_____

_____

_____

_____

_____

If I choose not to trust God and surrender to Him (I will continue doing what unwanted behavior?):

_____

_____

_____

_____

_____

If the right thing to do is the hard thing to do, what do you need to do? (Hint: Trusting God is the hard thing - so what fears or controls will you need to surrender to Him?)

_____

_____

_____

_____

_____

What are you willing to do this week in light of trusting God?

_____

_____

_____

_____

_____

_____

_____

_____

_____

_____

_____

_____

_____

_____

_____

_____

_____

_____

_____

_____

_____

_____

_____

As you read through this section about PTSD and discoveries made about troops with family of origin trauma and battlefield trauma, journal how your past and present traumas might be affecting you and your husband.

_____

_____

_____

_____

_____

_____

How do you see trauma in your life repeating itself? (Perhaps having to keep secrets as a child and having to keep secrets now; feeling abandoned or lied to as a child and feeling that way now).

_____

_____

_____

_____

_____

_____

After filling out your chart on Whacks and Lacks, think about what messages were communicated to you because of the whacks and lacks of life? **What are the statements that Hell has tried to use to bring you down?**

We will get to what God says about you. But to truly hear and receive words of grace and encouragement, you need to identify the lies that have been the background music of your soul for years.

EXAMPLES:

- I am not enough
- I have to prove myself
- Those closest to me will abandon me
- I have to protect myself, no one else will

1. _____

_____

2. _____

_____

3. _____

_____

4. _____

_____

What incident, event or comments do you struggle with most from your past?

_____

_____

_____

_____

How might your past trauma be affecting you in the present?

_____

_____

_____

_____

(icon) *Lesson Two*

TRAUMA'S INFLUENCE IN MY HEALING JOURNEY

Thought for the week: *It is valuable to take time to reflect upon the journey you have taken. You are on the path to healing from old wounds, while you are learning skills to help strengthen you. Courageously continue your journey!*

List five things you are thankful for this week.

1. _____

2. _____

3. _____

4. _____

5. _____

In your *Workbook*, if you checked three or more of the thirteen questions about your early childhood as true, journal what you discovered about you, the little girl.

_____

_____

_____

_____

_____

_____

_____

Meditate on this Scripture and journal your thoughts.

> *God's riches, wisdom, and knowledge are so deep*
> *that it is impossible to explain his decisions*
> *or to understand his ways.*
> *"Who knows how the Lord thinks?*
> *Who can become his adviser?"*
> *Who gave the Lord something*
> *which the Lord must pay back?*
> *Everything is from him and by him and for him.*
> *Glory belongs to him forever! Amen!*
>
> ROMANS 11:33-36 (GW)

_____

_____

_____

_____

_____

_____

Meditate on this statement and Scripture, especially in light of what you learned about Joseph's life, and ask God what this might mean in your life: God will even use adversity to position you for blessing…if you let Him!

> *You intended to harm me, but God intended it all for good.*
>
> GENESIS 50:20 (NLT)

_____

_____

_____

_____

_____

If you scored high in TRT, write a letter to one person who wounded you deeply from your past. Honestly share the hurt that you experienced from the actions and attitudes of this person. For now, we do not recommend you send the letter. While at some point you may want to send a revised version of this letter, the main purpose for now is for you to be able to express your pain and hurt without worrying about how it is worded, or how it might impact the other person. No need to write forgiveness to this person yet; you will have an opportunity to do that in a future lesson. Just write about your pain. As you will see from Anne's continued testimony in the next lesson, a new freedom came as she was able to express all the anger that she felt inside.

_____

_____

_____

_____

_____

_____

_____

_____

_____

_____

_____

_____

_____

_____

_____

_____

_____

_____

_____

Finally, of the categories from the Stress Index Answer Grid in which you scored three or more, identify how God has used these adversities to position you for blessing. Once you identify the blessing or potential blessing, you will disarm the power of trauma and hurt in your life. *(Example: I have learned to be much more compassionate to women who suffer from trauma.)*

A. _____

B. _____

C. _____

Lesson Three
GOD'S GRACE TRUMPS TRAUMA

Thought for the week: *Secrets keep us in the dark. Secrets make us sick. Bringing those secrets into the Light allows God's Grace to heal us, as we continue to respond to His call to move ever forward on our journey.*

List five things you are thankful for this week.

1. _____
2. _____
3. _____
4. _____
5. _____

In reviewing the Scripture in this week's lesson (Psalm 105:17-22), what pressures has God added to your life? How can you relate to the Israelites in their plight of having more straw taken away from them?

_____

_____

_____

Read through and meditate on Genesis 40-50. Write down why Joseph would have a legitimate cause to wrestle with ongoing injustices in his life.

_____

_____

⚓

In your *Workbook*, you were asked to write down the answer to this in your *Journal*. Consider one of the events under the TB category that you listed on your chart. When did you feel distress like this in your past?

_____

_____

_____

_____

Describe what you were feeling and some lies you might have believed at the time (e.g. fear of not being taken care of financially, anxiety over comparing myself to other women). If you feel stuck on this, pray for the Holy Spirit to give you insight. Further help from a pastor or counselor might be needed.

_____

_____

_____

_____

_____

_____

_____

_____

_____

_____

_____

_____

_____

How can you relate to Joseph's struggle?

_____

_____

_____

_____

Write a note to the child you once were and tell her it was okay to be terrified and confused by a traumatic event you experienced. Add any other comforting words you would like to have heard from an adult.

_____

_____

_____

_____

_____

_____

_____

_____

_____

_____

_____

_____

_____

_____

_____

_____

_____

⬜ *Lesson Four*

GETTING UNSTUCK FROM TRAUMA'S HOLD

Thought for the week: *We seem to have more compassion and understanding for the pain others feel than we do for our own woundedness. Would that we are able to treat ourselves with compassion as we face our own pain and shame.*

List five things you are thankful for this week.

1. _____

2. _____

3. _____

4. _____

5. _____

Write your trauma story from the perspective of an observer, using third person pronouns (e.g. she, her, they). You may use the pages that follow to write your story.

- Your Trauma Chart from Lesson Four can help you include significant elements for your story.

- Suggested length of your story: 700 words or less.

- Start your story with: "Once upon a time there was a little girl..."

- Read your story after it is completed. Write some journal notes at the end of the story about how you felt as you read about the little girl in your story.

- Be prepared to share it with ladies in your group the next time you meet.

Once upon a time there was a little girl…

_____

_____

_____

_____

_____

_____

_____

_____

_____

_____

_____

_____

_____

_____

_____

_____

_____

_____

_____

_____

_____

_____

_____

_____

Share how you felt about re-reading the story of your little girl.

_____

_____

_____

_____

_____

_____

_____

_____

After reading your trauma story to your group, write down how you felt.

_____

_____

_____

_____

_____

_____

_____

_____

_____

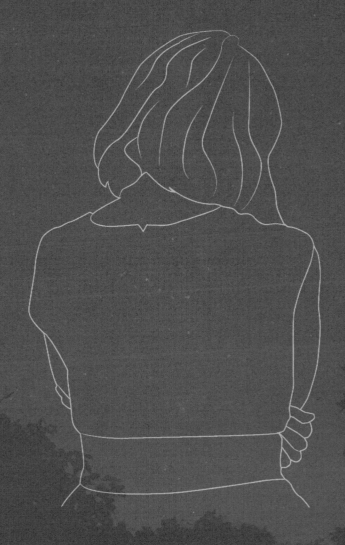

Chapter Five

UNTANGLING UNHEALTHY RELATIONSHIPS

Lesson One

IS IT TRAUMA OR CODEPENDENCY?

Thought for the week: Sometimes it's very difficult to determine our own motives. This is another reason we need healthy mentors around us: They can speak truth into our lives and help us better understand why we do the things we do.

List five things you are thankful for this week.

1. _____
2. _____
3. _____
4. _____
5. _____

In checking the categories in the chart with the motives of safety or control/enabling, write down what you discovered about yourself.

_____
_____
_____
_____
_____
_____
_____
_____
_____
_____

How have you suffered the consequences by rescuing?

_____

_____

_____

_____

Circle two of the statements on the Simple Codependency Checklist in your _Work-book_ that are the strongest for you. In the space below, describe the behavior you would like to see instead of the codependent behavior and share a first step you could take to make that change. We've included an example to help you.

CHECKLIST STATEMENT	DESIRED NEW BEHAVIORS, ATTITUDES, FOCUS	FIRST STEP
I read his journal	_I want to stop reading his journal_	_I will stop looking for his journal. When I see it, I will not touch it. If I have the desire to read it, I will call one of my fellow heroines._

Who will hold you accountable to take those first steps? _____

Lesson Three

LOSING YOURSELF BEHIND THE MASK

Thought for the week: To truly be known, we must put aside our masks and face the fear of rejection. This is yet another step on your journey toward the reward you seek.

List five things you are thankful for this week.

1. _____

2. _____

3. _____

4. _____

5. _____

In your *Workbook* this week you were asked to star the traits with which you most struggle. Now write about your childhood memories of learning one or more of the traits you starred.

_____

_____

_____

_____

_____

_____

_____

_____

_____

In your *Workbook* you were also asked to list the masks you have used to protect yourself in the past and in the present. Next to each you listed, share how old it is and what its job was.

THE MASK	AGE YOU BEGAN WEARING IT	ITS JOB - HOW DID IT PROTECT YOU?

What have you experienced as a result of wearing these masks?

_____

_____

How have they helped or hindered your life?

_____

_____

In the space below, journal the masks you identify during the week, worn by yourself and others. Circle the masks you identify as ones you wore this week.

_____

_____

_____

_____

(icon) Lesson Four

LIFTING THE MASK TO HEAL THE WOUNDS

Thought for the week: No matter what limbic lie we have believed, God always speaks to us in terms of His love, His acceptance, and His grace. Believe this truth: You are unconditionally loved by God!

List five things you are thankful for this week.

1. _____
2. _____
3. _____
4. _____
5. _____

Journal your thoughts about the lies you listed on the warped mirror.

_____
_____
_____
_____
_____
_____
_____
_____
_____
_____

Take one of those lies and ask God when it began. Ask Him who He says you are. Try to remember where and when you first thought that lie. Then picture Him coming in and picture what He would say and do, which is probably opposite of what you experienced. Remember, He despised the shame.

Write down all you saw and what He spoke to you.

_____

_____

_____

_____

_____

_____

_____

_____

_____

_____

_____

_____

_____

_____

_____

_____

_____

_____

_____

Now list who God says you are on your *Workbook* mirror. Do the same for every lie you listed.

After spending time with God to exchange the lie with a truth that God SHOWS you (a right brain experience), find a *logos* word either on your own or from this list that underlines what He has said:

WHO I AM IN CHRIST[4]
THE WORD OF GOD SAYS:

1. I am God's child for I am born again of the incorruptible seed of the Word of God that lives and abides forever. (1 Peter 1:23)

2. I am forgiven of all my sins and washed in the blood. (Ephesians 1:7; Hebrews 9:14; Colossians 1:14; 1 John 2:12; 1 John 1:9)

3. I am a new creation. (2 Corinthians 5:17)

4. I am a temple where the Holy Spirit lives. (1 Corinthians 6:19)

5. I am delivered from the power of darkness; Christ brings me into God's kingdom. (Colossians 1:13)

6. I am redeemed from the curse of the law. (1 Peter 1:18-19)

7. I am holy and without blame before God. (Ephesians 1:4)

8. I am established to the end. (1 Corinthians 1:8)

9. I am close to God - brought closer through the blood of Christ. (Ephesians 2:13)

10. I am victorious. (Revelation 21:7)

11. I am set free. (John 8:31-32)

12. I am strong in the Lord. (Ephesians 6:10)

13. I am dead to sin. (Romans 6:2 & 11; 1 Peter 2:24)

14. I am more than a conqueror. (Romans 8:37)

15. I am a co-heir with Christ. (Romans 8:16-17)

16. I am sealed with the Holy Spirit of promise. (Ephesians 1:13)

17. I am in Christ Jesus by His doing. (1 Corinthians 1:30)

18. I am accepted in Jesus Christ. (Ephesians 1:5-6)

19. I am complete in Him. (Colossians 2:10)

....

4. Ted Roberts, *Living Life Boldly Study Guide* (Gresham, OR: East Hill Church, 2005) 75-76. Used by permission.

As a review, write down some of the self discovering truths you have made about:

1. The truth of your spouse's addiction (it is not about you)

_____

_____

_____

_____

2. The powerful influence of your family of origin

_____

_____

_____

_____

3. The power of trauma and possible codependent behaviors to acquire safety

_____

_____

_____

_____

In light of Beth's story about steel in her bones, how might your promises help you with the betrayal you have experienced?

_____

_____

_____

_____

As you look at the FASTER Scale, figure out one or two areas you tend to slip to and hang out. Then meditate on the Scripture for that area and comment on how the truth of that could help you this week. You may want to come back to these Scriptures in future lessons when you find yourself somewhere else on the FASTER Scale.

FORGETTING PRIORITIES

> *Jesus replied: "'Love the Lord your God with all your heart and with all your soul and with all your mind.' This is the first and greatest commandment. And the second is like it: 'Love your neighbor as yourself.'"*
>
> MATTHEW 22:37-39 (NIV)

_____

_____

_____

_____

_____

ANXIETY

> *Do not be anxious about anything, but in every situation, by prayer and petition, with thanksgiving, present your requests to God. And the peace of God, which transcends all understanding, will guard your hearts and your minds in Christ Jesus.*
>
> PHILIPPIANS 4:6-7 (NIV)

_____

_____

_____

_____

_____

_____

SPEEDING UP

He says, "Be still, and know that I am God; I will be exalted among the nations,
I will be exalted in the earth."

PSALM 46:10 (NIV)

"The Lord your God is with you, the Mighty Warrior who saves.
He will take great delight in you; in his love he will no longer rebuke you,
but will rejoice over you with singing."

ZEPHANIAH 3:17 (NIV)

_____

_____

_____

_____

_____

TICKED OFF

"In your anger do not sin": Do not let the sun go down while you are still angry,
and do not give the devil a foothold.

EPHESIANS 4:26-27 (NIV)

_____

_____

_____

_____

_____

_____

EXHAUSTED

Then Jesus said, "Come to me, all of you who are weary and carry heavy burdens, and I will give you rest. Take my yoke upon you. Let me teach you, because I am humble and gentle at heart, and you will find rest for your souls. For my yoke is easy to bear, and the burden I give you is light."

MATTHEW 11:28-30 (NLT)

_____

_____

_____

_____

RELAPSE

Be very careful, then, how you live—not as unwise but as wise, making the most of every opportunity, because the days are evil. Therefore do not be foolish, but understand what the Lord's will is. Do not get drunk on wine, which leads to debauchery. Instead, be filled with the Spirit,

EPHESIANS 5:15-18 (NIV)

_____

_____

_____

COURAGEOUS COMMITMENT TO CHANGE

☐ I will give thanks each day

☐ I will rehearse my promises

☐ I will call three women this week

☐ I will share my FASTER Scale & Double Bind this week

Who will hold you accountable? _____

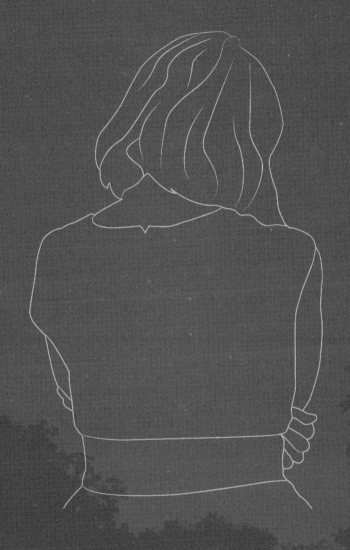

Chapter Six

HEALTHY BOUNDARIES

Lesson One

STEPS TO THE NEW DANCE: BOUNDARIES

Thought for the week: *We get to choose whom we allow access to our lives, and how much access to allow them. God grants us that right and responsibility. Establishing healthy boundaries helps us establish healthy relationships with others.*

List five things you are thankful for this week.

1. _____
2. _____
3. _____
4. _____
5. _____

Write down the personal/prophetic promises God has shown you so far with the Scripture He has given you.

1. _____
   _____

2. _____
   _____

3. _____
   _____

4. _____
   _____

Previous week's commitment - How did I do?

_____

_____

_____

_____

Share a current personal situation that you are involved in that would demonstrate boundary violations.

_____

_____

_____

_____

_____

_____

What Scripture meant the most to you as you studied your _Workbook_ lesson this week? Explain.

_____

_____

_____

_____

_____

_____

How has God respected my boundaries? Do I allow Him into my life or leave Him at the door?

_____

_____

_____

_____

Who did you list as people who have good boundaries? Consider writing a letter to them, thanking them for that healthy experience. If you didn't have someone in your life to model those healthy boundaries, write out a prayer asking God to bring them into your life.

_____

_____

_____

_____

_____

Since learning to set healthy boundaries is such an important new dance step, write out a prayer asking God to open your heart and mind to begin to see boundaries from His perspective. Let Him know that you are willing to see where you have stepped on others' toes and make changes.

_____

_____

_____

_____

Next week you will be sharing how you worked on your Courageous Commitment to Change and your FASTER Scale. This will become a weekly exercise.

COURAGEOUS COMMITMENT TO CHANGE

1. What area do you need to change or what challenge are you facing next week?

_____

_____

2. What will it cost you emotionally if you do change? What fear will you have to face?

_____

_____

3. What will it cost you if you don't change?

_____

_____

4. What is your plan to maintain your restoration regarding these changes?

_____

_____

5. Who will keep you accountable to this commitment?

Name _____   Day _____

Name _____   Day _____

Name _____   Day _____

6. What are the details of your accountability this week? What questions should they ask?

_____

_____

_____

FASTER SCALE

Adapted with permission from the *Genesis Process* by Michael Dye

PART ONE

Circle the behaviors on the FASTER Scale that you identify with in each section.

....

Restoration – (**Accepting life on God's terms, with trust, grace, mercy, vulnerability and gratitude.**) No current secrets; working to resolve problems; identifying fears and feelings; keeping commitments to meetings, prayer, family, church, people, goals, and self; being open and honest, making eye contact; increasing in relationships with God and others; true accountability.

....

Forgetting Priorities – (**Start believing the present circumstances and moving away from trusting God. Denial; flight; a change in what's important; how you spend your time, energy, and thoughts.**) Secrets; less time/energy for God, meetings, church; avoiding support and accountability people; superficial conversations; sarcasm; isolating; changes in goals; obsessed with relationships; breaking promises & commitments; neglecting family; preoccupation with material things, TV, computers, entertainment; procrastination; lying; overconfidence; bored; hiding money; image management; seeking to control situations and other people.

....

Forgetting Priorities will lead to the inclusion of:

Anxiety – (**A growing background noise of undefined fear; getting energy from emotions.**) Worry, using profanity, being fearful; being resentful; replaying old, negative thoughts; perfectionism; judging other's motives; making goals and lists that you can't complete; mind reading; fantasy, codependent, rescuing; sleep problems, trouble concentrating, seeking/creating drama; gossip; using over-the-counter medication for pain, sleep or weight control; flirting.

....

Anxiety then leads to the inclusion of:

Speeding Up – **(Trying to outrun the anxiety which is usually the first sign of depression.)** Super busy and always in a hurry (finding good reason to justify the work); workaholic; can't relax; avoiding slowing down; feeling driven; can't turn off thoughts; skipping meals; binge eating (usually at night); overspending; can't identify own feelings/needs; repetitive negative thoughts; irritable; dramatic mood swings; too much caffeine; over exercising; nervousness; difficulty being alone and/or with people; difficulty listening to others; making excuses for having to "do it all."

....

Speeding Up then leads to the inclusion of:

Ticked Off – **(Getting adrenaline high on anger and aggression.)** Procrastination causing crisis in money, work, and relationships; increased sarcasm; black and white (all or nothing) thinking; feeling alone; nobody understands; overreacting, road rage; constant resentments; pushing others away; increasing isolation; blaming; arguing; irrational thinking; can't take criticism; defensive; people avoiding you; needing to be right; digestive problems; headaches; obsessive (stuck) thoughts; can't forgive; feeling superior; using intimidation.

....

Ticked Off then leads to the inclusion of:

Exhausted – **(Loss of physical and emotional energy; coming off the adrenaline high, and the onset of depression.)** Depressed; panicked; confused; hopelessness; sleeping too much or too little; can't cope; overwhelmed; crying for "no reason"; can't think; forgetful; pessimistic; helpless; tired; numb; wanting to run; constant cravings for old coping behaviors; thinking of using sex, drugs, or alcohol; seeking old unhealthy people & places; really isolating; people angry with you; self abuse; suicidal thoughts; spontaneous crying; no goals; survival mode; not returning phone calls; missing work; irritability; no appetite.

....

Exhausted then leads to the inclusion of:

Relapse – **(Returning to the place you swore you would never go again. Coping with life on your terms. You sitting in the driver's seat instead of God.)** Giving up and giving in; out of control; lost in your addiction; lying to yourself and others; feeling you just can't manage without your coping behaviors, at least for now. The result is the reinforcement of shame, guilt and condemnation; and feelings of abandonment and being alone.

....

PART TWO

Identify the most powerful behavior in each section and write it next to the corresponding heading.

Answer the following three questions:

1. How does it affect me? How do I feel in the moment?
2. How does it affect the important people in my life?
3. Why do I do this? What is the benefit for me?

Restoration: _____

1. _____
2. _____
3. _____

Forgetting Priorities: _____

1. _____
2. _____
3. _____

Anxiety: _____

1. _____
2. _____
3. _____

Speeding Up: _____

1. _____
2. _____
3. _____

Ticked Off: _____

1. _____
2. _____
3. _____

Exhausted: _____

1. _____
2. _____
3. _____

Relapse: _____

1. _____
2. _____
3. _____

GROUP CHECK-IN
COMPLETE 24 HOURS BEFORE GROUP

1. What is the lowest level you reached on the **FASTER Scale** this week?

_____

2. What was the **Double Bind** you were dealing with?

_____

_____

_____

_____

3. Where are you on your **Courageous Commitment to Change** from our last meeting?

_____

4. What information from your Betrayal & Beyond lesson was most applicable to your situation this week? What information had the most impact emotionally?

_____

_____

_____

5. What have you done to improve your relationship with your husband or other significant relationships this week?

_____

_____

_____

⧉ Lesson Two
STEPS TO THE NEW DANCE: BALANCE

Thought for the week: As this journey progresses, at times you may feel overwhelmed with the amount of information you must process. This heroine's journey is hard work. The alternative to moving forward, however, is moving backward. You've come too far to go back now. Press on!

List five things you are thankful for this week.

1. _____

2. _____

3. _____

4. _____

5. _____

List the personal/prophetic promises that God has shown you so far with the Scripture He has given you.

1. _____
_____

2. _____
_____

3. _____
_____

4. _____
_____

DOUBLE BIND EXERCISE FOR OVERFUNCTIONING

Double Bind on the most problematic behavior you listed for overfunctioning:

_____

_____

Begin to work through and record your answers to this Double Bind exercise based on the area you selected.

How will continuing in this behavior affect your relationships? For example, if control is your issue, your answer might look something like this: _There will be no change in the addict becoming responsible for himself._

_____

_____

...at are the fears you might have to face? For ...ill relapse.

_____

_____

...ce), what is one small thing you could do to-
...establish a healthy boundary such as, "I am no
...n when it comes to the computer. I need you
...you use." (Covenant Eyes informs his account-
...regular basis. To learn more about accountabil-
...tability App User's Guide from puredesire.org/
...ep:

_____

_____

...through on this first step? _____

After identifying the violation(s) and the fear for underfunctioning, it is again important to go through the Double Bind exercise.

DOUBLE BIND EXERCISE FOR UNDERFUNCTIONING

If I continue allowing these violations to take place, what will happen?

_____

_____

_____

_____

_____

If I do confront these violations, what fears will I need to face?

_____

_____

_____

_____

_____

If I do the hard thing and face my fear, what is one thing I could do toward making changes so I am no longer a victim of these violations?

_____

_____

_____

_____

_____

Who will keep me accountable? _____

Journal your reactions to completing the Abuse Inventory in this lesson.

_____

_____

_____

_____

_____

_____

_____

_____

_____

_____

Meditate on these Scriptures: Isaiah 43:1-3 and Deuteronomy 31:8. Consider God's presence in your life in spite of the abuse.

_____

_____

_____

_____

_____

_____

_____

_____

_____

_____

COURAGEOUS COMMITMENT TO CHANGE

1. What area do you need to change or what challenge are you facing next week?

_____

_____

2. What will it cost you emotionally if you do change? What fear will you have to face?

_____

_____

3. What will it cost you if you don't change?

_____

_____

4. What is your plan to maintain your restoration regarding these changes?

_____

_____

5. Who will keep you accountable to this commitment?

Name _____ Day _____

Name _____ Day _____

Name _____ Day _____

6. What are the details of your accountability this week? What questions should they ask?

_____

_____

_____

FASTER SCALE

Adapted with permission from the *Genesis Process* by Michael Dye

PART ONE

Circle the behaviors on the FASTER Scale that you identify with in each section.

....

Restoration – (**Accepting life on God's terms, with trust, grace, mercy, vulnerability and gratitude.**) No current secrets; working to resolve problems; identifying fears and feelings; keeping commitments to meetings, prayer, family, church, people, goals, and self; being open and honest, making eye contact; increasing in relationships with God and others; true accountability.

....

Forgetting Priorities – (**Start believing the present circumstances and moving away from trusting God. Denial; flight; a change in what's important; how you spend your time, energy, and thoughts.**) Secrets; less time/energy for God, meetings, church; avoiding support and accountability people; superficial conversations; sarcasm; isolating; changes in goals; obsessed with relationships; breaking promises & commitments; neglecting family; preoccupation with material things, TV, computers, entertainment; procrastination; lying; overconfidence; bored; hiding money; image management; seeking to control situations and other people.

....

Forgetting Priorities will lead to the inclusion of:

Anxiety – (**A growing background noise of undefined fear; getting energy from emotions.**) Worry, using profanity, being fearful; being resentful; replaying old, negative thoughts; perfectionism; judging other's motives; making goals and lists that you can't complete; mind reading; fantasy, codependent, rescuing; sleep problems, trouble concentrating, seeking/creating drama; gossip; using over-the-counter medication for pain, sleep or weight control; flirting.

....

119

Anxiety then leads to the inclusion of:

Speeding Up – **(Trying to outrun the anxiety which is usually the first sign of depression.)** Super busy and always in a hurry (finding good reason to justify the work); workaholic; can't relax; avoiding slowing down; feeling driven; can't turn off thoughts; skipping meals; binge eating (usually at night); overspending; can't identify own feelings/needs; repetitive negative thoughts; irritable; dramatic mood swings; too much caffeine; over exercising; nervousness; difficulty being alone and/or with people; difficulty listening to others; making excuses for having to "do it all."

....

Speeding Up then leads to the inclusion of:

Ticked Off – **(Getting adrenaline high on anger and aggression.)** Procrastination causing crisis in money, work, and relationships; increased sarcasm; black and white (all or nothing) thinking; feeling alone; nobody understands; overreacting, road rage; constant resentments; pushing others away; increasing isolation; blaming; arguing; irrational thinking; can't take criticism; defensive; people avoiding you; needing to be right; digestive problems; headaches; obsessive (stuck) thoughts; can't forgive; feeling superior; using intimidation.

....

Ticked Off then leads to the inclusion of:

Exhausted – **(Loss of physical and emotional energy; coming off the adrenaline high, and the onset of depression.)** Depressed; panicked; confused; hopelessness; sleeping too much or too little; can't cope; overwhelmed; crying for "no reason"; can't think; forgetful; pessimistic; helpless; tired; numb; wanting to run; constant cravings for old coping behaviors; thinking of using sex, drugs, or alcohol; seeking old unhealthy people & places; really isolating; people angry with you; self abuse; suicidal thoughts; spontaneous crying; no goals; survival mode; not returning phone calls; missing work; irritability; no appetite.

....

Exhausted then leads to the inclusion of:

Relapse – **(Returning to the place you swore you would never go again. Coping with life on your terms. You sitting in the driver's seat instead of God.)** Giving up and giving in; out of control; lost in your addiction; lying to yourself and others; feeling you just can't manage without your coping behaviors, at least for now. The result is the reinforcement of shame, guilt and condemnation; and feelings of abandonment and being alone.

....

PART TWO

Identify the most powerful behavior in each section and write it next to the corresponding heading.

Answer the following three questions:
1. How does it affect me? How do I feel in the moment?
2. How does it affect the important people in my life?
3. Why do I do this? What is the benefit for me?

Restoration: _____
1. _____
2. _____
3. _____

Forgetting Priorities: _____
1. _____
2. _____
3. _____

Anxiety: _____
1. _____
2. _____
3. _____

Speeding Up: _____
1. _____
2. _____
3. _____

Ticked Off: _____
1. _____
2. _____
3. _____

Exhausted: _____
1. _____
2. _____
3. _____

Relapse: _____
1. _____
2. _____
3. _____

GROUP CHECK-IN
COMPLETE 24 HOURS BEFORE GROUP

1. What is the lowest level you reached on the **FASTER Scale** this week?

_____

2. What was the **Double Bind** you were dealing with?

_____

_____

_____

_____

3. Where are you on your **Courageous Commitment to Change** from our last meeting?

_____

4. What information from your Betrayal & Beyond lesson was most applicable to your situation this week? What information had the most impact emotionally?

_____

_____

_____

5. What have you done to improve your relationship with your husband or other significant relationships this week?

_____

_____

_____

Lesson Three

STEPS TO THE NEW DANCE: MY SAFETY PLAN

Thought for the week: *The tools you are learning are critical for your own restoration; continue to practice them. The support of your mentor and your fellow heroines is also critical; continue to reach out and develop healthy relationships.*

List five things you are thankful for this week.

1. _____
2. _____
3. _____
4. _____
5. _____

List the personal/prophetic promises that God has shown you so far with the Scripture He has given you.

1. _____
   _____
2. _____
   _____
3. _____
   _____
4. _____
   _____

This week you will be working on your Safety Plan. Your leader will help you through this process. Please fill out your copy in your *Workbook* for this week and call some of the women in your group, sharing ideas and suggestions with each other. This will help you keep a balanced perspective in putting your Safety Plan together. The first step is very important because it says to your husband you are committed to the process. With the second step, try and choose only the things you need right now for your spouse to commit to. Many of the options may not reflect where your relationship is at this point.

You can fill out the Safety Plan in your *Workbook* for your own use and reference. When it comes time to share your Safety Plan with your spouse, go to puredesire.org/bb-resources, download and print the appropriate Safety Plan, fill it out, and give it to your husband.

It is recommended that you review your plan every six months and eliminate those items or action steps that no longer apply and add new ones (i.e. a marriage seminar might be appropriate after you both have finished a year in Pure Desire groups.)

Also included in the *Workbook* appendix on page 300 is a Couple's Safety Plan. We will talk further about that as we finish the final chapters of this book.

Journal your thoughts and feelings about doing your Safety Plan.

_____

_____

_____

_____

_____

_____

_____

_____

_____

_____

_____

_____

Write out a prayer asking God to help you with the timing and approach to sharing your Safety Plan. You might need a pastor, counselor or couple who has been through this process to be with you as you share. Part of your prayer could be asking God to prepare your husband's heart to receive what you will be sharing.

COURAGEOUS COMMITMENT TO CHANGE

1. What area do you need to change or what challenge are you facing next week?

_____

_____

2. What will it cost you emotionally if you do change? What fear will you have to face?

_____

_____

3. What will it cost you if you don't change?

_____

_____

4. What is your plan to maintain your restoration regarding these changes?

_____

_____

5. Who will keep you accountable to this commitment?

Name _____ Day _____

Name _____ Day _____

Name _____ Day _____

6. What are the details of your accountability this week? What questions should they ask?

_____

_____

_____

FASTER SCALE

Adapted with permission from the *Genesis Process* by Michael Dye

PART ONE

Circle the behaviors on the FASTER Scale that you identify with in each section.

....

Restoration – (**Accepting life on God's terms, with trust, grace, mercy, vulnerability and gratitude**.) No current secrets; working to resolve problems; identifying fears and feelings; keeping commitments to meetings, prayer, family, church, people, goals, and self; being open and honest, making eye contact; increasing in relationships with God and others; true accountability.

....

Forgetting Priorities – (**Start believing the present circumstances and moving away from trusting God. Denial; flight; a change in what's important; how you spend your time, energy, and thoughts.**) Secrets; less time/energy for God, meetings, church; avoiding support and accountability people; superficial conversations; sarcasm; isolating; changes in goals; obsessed with relationships; breaking promises & commitments; neglecting family; preoccupation with material things, TV, computers, entertainment; procrastination; lying; overconfidence; bored; hiding money; image management; seeking to control situations and other people.

....

Forgetting Priorities will lead to the inclusion of:

Anxiety – (**A growing background noise of undefined fear; getting energy from emotions.**) Worry, using profanity, being fearful; being resentful; replaying old, negative thoughts; perfectionism; judging other's motives; making goals and lists that you can't complete; mind reading; fantasy, codependent, rescuing; sleep problems, trouble concentrating, seeking/creating drama; gossip; using over-the-counter medication for pain, sleep or weight control; flirting.

....

Anxiety then leads to the inclusion of:

Speeding Up – (**Trying to outrun the anxiety which is usually the first sign of depression.**) Super busy and always in a hurry (finding good reason to justify the work); workaholic; can't relax; avoiding slowing down; feeling driven; can't turn off thoughts; skipping meals; binge eating (usually at night); overspending; can't identify own feelings/needs; repetitive negative thoughts; irritable; dramatic mood swings; too much caffeine; over exercising; nervousness; difficulty being alone and/or with people; difficulty listening to others; making excuses for having to "do it all."

....

Speeding Up then leads to the inclusion of:

Ticked Off – (**Getting adrenaline high on anger and aggression.**) Procrastination causing crisis in money, work, and relationships; increased sarcasm; black and white (all or nothing) thinking; feeling alone; nobody understands; overreacting, road rage; constant resentments; pushing others away; increasing isolation; blaming; arguing; irrational thinking; can't take criticism; defensive; people avoiding you; needing to be right; digestive problems; headaches; obsessive (stuck) thoughts; can't forgive; feeling superior; using intimidation.

....

Ticked Off then leads to the inclusion of:

Exhausted – (**Loss of physical and emotional energy; coming off the adrenaline high, and the onset of depression**.) Depressed; panicked; confused; hopelessness; sleeping too much or too little; can't cope; overwhelmed; crying for "no reason"; can't think; forgetful; pessimistic; helpless; tired; numb; wanting to run; constant cravings for old coping behaviors; thinking of using sex, drugs, or alcohol; seeking old unhealthy people & places; really isolating; people angry with you; self abuse; suicidal thoughts; spontaneous crying; no goals; survival mode; not returning phone calls; missing work; irritability; no appetite.

....

Exhausted then leads to the inclusion of:

Relapse – (**Returning to the place you swore you would never go again. Coping with life on your terms. You sitting in the driver's seat instead of God.**) Giving up and giving in; out of control; lost in your addiction; lying to yourself and others; feeling you just can't manage without your coping behaviors, at least for now. The result is the reinforcement of shame, guilt and condemnation; and feelings of abandonment and being alone.

....

PART TWO

Identify the most powerful behavior in each section and write it next to the corresponding heading.

Answer the following three questions:
1. How does it affect me? How do I feel in the moment?
2. How does it affect the important people in my life?
3. Why do I do this? What is the benefit for me?

Restoration: _____

1. _____
2. _____
3. _____

Forgetting Priorities: _____

1. _____
2. _____
3. _____

Anxiety: _____

1. _____
2. _____
3. _____

Speeding Up: _____

1. _____
2. _____
3. _____

Ticked Off: _____

1. _____
2. _____
3. _____

Exhausted: _____

1. _____
2. _____
3. _____

Relapse: _____

1. _____
2. _____
3. _____

GROUP CHECK-IN
COMPLETE 24 HOURS BEFORE GROUP

1. What is the lowest level you reached on the **FASTER Scale** this week?

_____

2. What was the **Double Bind** you were dealing with?

_____

_____

_____

_____

3. Where are you on your **Courageous Commitment to Change** from our last meeting?

_____

4. What information from your Betrayal & Beyond lesson was most applicable to your situation this week? What information had the most impact emotionally?

_____

_____

_____

5. What have you done to improve your relationship with your husband or other significant relationships this week?

_____

_____

_____

⊜ 𝓛𝑒𝓈𝓈𝑜𝓃 𝓕𝑜𝓊𝓇

STEPPING OUT WITH NEW DANCE MOVES

Thought for the week: *Experiencing the natural consequences of our bad behavior brings pain. Pain motivates us to change that bad behavior.*

List five things you are thankful for this week.

1. _____
2. _____
3. _____
4. _____
5. _____

Write down the personal/prophetic promises God has shown you so far with the Scripture He has given you.

1. _____
   _____

2. _____
   _____

3. _____
   _____

4. _____
   _____

Read the short book of Esther and journal your thoughts:

- About her Double Bind

_____

_____

_____

_____

_____

_____

- Her wisdom in approaching her husband

_____

_____

_____

_____

_____

- How God was faithful to Esther and her people

_____

_____

_____

_____

_____

What are you willing to risk to trust God to intervene on your behalf?

Think about the issues you are facing and list the hardest things you have difficulty relinquishing. These should be actions and consequences you have rescued your spouse from. Use this chart to help you do the Double Bind exercise which follows:

ISSUE	IF I RESCUE...	BUT IF I LET THE CONSE-QUENCES COME...	IMPACT ON HIM	IMPACT ON ME
Example: He is in charge of finances, but keeps getting charged late fees for not paying on time.	I could take charge and pay the bills on time, but he won't learn to be responsible.	He pays late charges with his coffee or lunch money.	There would be motivation on his part if he realized he would have to go without his coffee or lunch.	I might still be anxious, but would have to trust the natural consequences.

Journal your fears and feelings about trusting God in one or all of the areas you listed.

_____

_____

_____

_____

_____

If you choose to do the hard thing, what is one step you could take that would help you follow through with the natural consequences?

_____

_____

_____

_____

_____

Write out a prayer asking for God's courage and help, as Esther did in her time of crisis.

_____

_____

_____

_____

_____

_____

Share how you relate to the illustrations of the teeter-totter.

_____

_____

_____

_____

_____

_____

Write down which stage you find yourself at right now? Explain why.

_____

_____

_____

_____

_____

_____

_____

What do you need from God while at this stage on the teeter-totter?

_____

_____

_____

_____

_____

_____

COURAGEOUS COMMITMENT TO CHANGE

1. What area do you need to change or what challenge are you facing next week?

_____

_____

2. What will it cost you emotionally if you do change? What fear will you have to face?

_____

_____

3. What will it cost you if you don't change?

_____

_____

4. What is your plan to maintain your restoration regarding these changes?

_____

_____

5. Who will keep you accountable to this commitment?

Name _____   Day _____

Name _____   Day _____

Name _____   Day _____

6. What are the details of your accountability this week? What questions should they ask?

_____

_____

_____

FASTER SCALE

Adapted with permission from the *Genesis Process* by Michael Dye

PART ONE

Circle the behaviors on the FASTER Scale that you identify with in each section.

....

Restoration – (**Accepting life on God's terms, with trust, grace, mercy, vulnerability and gratitude.**) No current secrets; working to resolve problems; identifying fears and feelings; keeping commitments to meetings, prayer, family, church, people, goals, and self; being open and honest, making eye contact; increasing in relationships with God and others; true accountability.

....

Forgetting Priorities – (**Start believing the present circumstances and moving away from trusting God. Denial; flight; a change in what's important; how you spend your time, energy, and thoughts.**) Secrets; less time/energy for God, meetings, church; avoiding support and accountability people; superficial conversations; sarcasm; isolating; changes in goals; obsessed with relationships; breaking promises & commitments; neglecting family; preoccupation with material things, TV, computers, entertainment; procrastination; lying; overconfidence; bored; hiding money; image management; seeking to control situations and other people.

....

Forgetting Priorities will lead to the inclusion of:

Anxiety – (**A growing background noise of undefined fear; getting energy from emotions.**) Worry, using profanity, being fearful; being resentful; replaying old, negative thoughts; perfectionism; judging other's motives; making goals and lists that you can't complete; mind reading; fantasy, codependent, rescuing; sleep problems, trouble concentrating, seeking/creating drama; gossip; using over-the-counter medication for pain, sleep or weight control; flirting.

....

137

Anxiety then leads to the inclusion of:

Speeding Up – **(Trying to outrun the anxiety which is usually the first sign of depression.)** Super busy and always in a hurry (finding good reason to justify the work); workaholic; can't relax; avoiding slowing down; feeling driven; can't turn off thoughts; skipping meals; binge eating (usually at night); overspending; can't identify own feelings/needs; repetitive negative thoughts; irritable; dramatic mood swings; too much caffeine; over exercising; nervousness; difficulty being alone and/or with people; difficulty listening to others; making excuses for having to "do it all."

....

Speeding Up then leads to the inclusion of:

Ticked Off – **(Getting adrenaline high on anger and aggression.)** Procrastination causing crisis in money, work, and relationships; increased sarcasm; black and white (all or nothing) thinking; feeling alone; nobody understands; overreacting, road rage; constant resentments; pushing others away; increasing isolation; blaming; arguing; irrational thinking; can't take criticism; defensive; people avoiding you; needing to be right; digestive problems; headaches; obsessive (stuck) thoughts; can't forgive; feeling superior; using intimidation.

....

Ticked Off then leads to the inclusion of:

Exhausted – **(Loss of physical and emotional energy; coming off the adrenaline high, and the onset of depression.)** Depressed; panicked; confused; hopelessness; sleeping too much or too little; can't cope; overwhelmed; crying for "no reason"; can't think; forgetful; pessimistic; helpless; tired; numb; wanting to run; constant cravings for old coping behaviors; thinking of using sex, drugs, or alcohol; seeking old unhealthy people & places; really isolating; people angry with you; self abuse; suicidal thoughts; spontaneous crying; no goals; survival mode; not returning phone calls; missing work; irritability; no appetite.

....

Exhausted then leads to the inclusion of:

Relapse – **(Returning to the place you swore you would never go again. Coping with life on your terms. You sitting in the driver's seat instead of God.)** Giving up and giving in; out of control; lost in your addiction; lying to yourself and others; feeling you just can't manage without your coping behaviors, at least for now. The result is the reinforcement of shame, guilt and condemnation; and feelings of abandonment and being alone.

....

PART TWO

Identify the most powerful behavior in each section and write it next to the corresponding heading.

Answer the following three questions:
1. How does it affect me? How do I feel in the moment?
2. How does it affect the important people in my life?
3. Why do I do this? What is the benefit for me?

Restoration: _____
1. _____
2. _____
3. _____

Forgetting Priorities: _____
1. _____
2. _____
3. _____

Anxiety: _____
1. _____
2. _____
3. _____

Speeding Up: _____
1. _____
2. _____
3. _____

Ticked Off: _____
1. _____
2. _____
3. _____

Exhausted: _____
1. _____
2. _____
3. _____

Relapse: _____
1. _____
2. _____
3. _____

GROUP CHECK-IN
COMPLETE 24 HOURS BEFORE GROUP

1. What is the lowest level you reached on the **FASTER Scale** this week?

_____

2. What was the **Double Bind** you were dealing with?

_____

_____

_____

_____

3. Where are you on your **Courageous Commitment to Change** from our last meeting?

_____

4. What information from your Betrayal & Beyond lesson was most applicable to your situation this week? What information had the most impact emotionally?

_____

_____

_____

5. What have you done to improve your relationship with your husband or other significant relationships this week?

_____

_____

_____

THE COURAGEOUS ROAD TO RESTORATION

You have come so far on your *heroine's journey*. In deciding to accept your Call to Adventure, in meeting with and accepting assistance from your Betrayal & Beyond group members, and in confronting the series of obstacles and challenges you have had to face you have gained greater knowledge and insight about trauma and sex addiction, and have learned new tools that are helping you emerge from this battle as a stronger, healthier person.

Perhaps your marriage is stronger than ever; perhaps there are still many issues to confront. Perhaps, sadly, your marriage has not survived this journey. Whichever your reality, as you continue on your journey you will be challenged to move forward, toward your reward of a new, upgraded *status quo*. During this part of your journey, you will begin to see what God can do as you accept the challenge of facing your losses, your anger, and your hurts head-on.

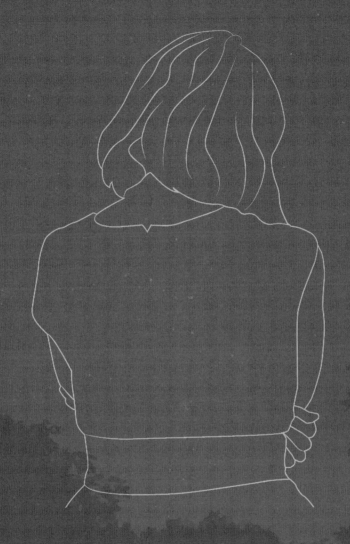

Chapter Seven

FACING MY GRIEF AND ANGER

⬡ 📄 *Lesson One*

THE STAGES OF GRIEF

Thought for the week: As you continue on this Journey, remember that only through some sort of great loss can a heroine gain the insight necessary to fulfill her destiny, or to reach her journey's end. Continue your Courageous Journey.

List five things you are thankful for this week.

1. _____
2. _____
3. _____
4. _____
5. _____

Write down the personal/prophetic promises God has shown you so far with the Scripture He has given you.

1. _____
   _____

2. _____
   _____

3. _____
   _____

4. _____
   _____

In Chapter 4, Lesson 3 we looked at Joseph's life and how he was impacted by trauma. Meditate on the Scripture that gives us a snapshot of his life:

> *He [God] sent a man ahead of them [Jacob's family].*
> *He sent Joseph, who was sold as a slave.*
> *They hurt his feet with shackles and cut into his neck with an iron collar.*
> *The LORD's promise tested him through fiery trials until his prediction came true.*
> *The king sent someone to release him.*
> *The ruler of nations set him free.*
> *He made Joseph the master of his palace and the ruler of all his possessions.*
> *Joseph trained the king's officers the way he wanted*
> *and taught his respected leaders wisdom.*
>
> PSALM 105:17-22 (GW)

Joseph would have listed the following losses he needed to grieve:

- Loss of safety and trust when his brothers threatened to kill him.

- Loss of his freedom when his brothers sold him into slavery.

- Loss of his family and his country when he was taken to Egypt.

- Loss of his freedom again when he was put into prison because of false accusations.

Looking back at Psalm 105, how did God take what the enemy meant for harm and turn it to Joseph's good, as well as good for the generations to come?

_____

_____

_____

_____

_____

_____

_____

_____

_____

As you are grieving over your own losses, how might Joseph's story encourage you?

_____

_____

_____

_____

_____

_____

_____

_____

_____

_____

Write out your thoughts about the Stockdale Paradox and how that applies to your life.

_____

_____

_____

_____

_____

_____

_____

_____

_____

_____

_____

_____

COURAGEOUS COMMITMENT TO CHANGE

1. What area do you need to change or what challenge are you facing next week?

_____

_____

2. What will it cost you emotionally if you do change? What fear will you have to face?

_____

_____

3. What will it cost you if you don't change?

_____

_____

4. What is your plan to maintain your restoration regarding these changes?

_____

_____

5. Who will keep you accountable to this commitment?

Name _____   Day _____

Name _____   Day _____

Name _____   Day _____

6. What are the details of your accountability this week? What questions should they ask?

_____

_____

_____

FASTER SCALE

Adapted with permission from the *Genesis Process* by Michael Dye

PART ONE

Circle the behaviors on the FASTER Scale that you identify with in each section.

....

Restoration – (**Accepting life on God's terms, with trust, grace, mercy, vulnerability and gratitude.**) No current secrets; working to resolve problems; identifying fears and feelings; keeping commitments to meetings, prayer, family, church, people, goals, and self; being open and honest, making eye contact; increasing in relationships with God and others; true accountability.

....

Forgetting Priorities – (**Start believing the present circumstances and moving away from trusting God. Denial; flight; a change in what's important; how you spend your time, energy, and thoughts.**) Secrets; less time/energy for God, meetings, church; avoiding support and accountability people; superficial conversations; sarcasm; isolating; changes in goals; obsessed with relationships; breaking promises & commitments; neglecting family; preoccupation with material things, TV, computers, entertainment; procrastination; lying; overconfidence; bored; hiding money; image management; seeking to control situations and other people.

....

Forgetting Priorities will lead to the inclusion of:

Anxiety – (**A growing background noise of undefined fear; getting energy from emotions.**) Worry, using profanity, being fearful; being resentful; replaying old, negative thoughts; perfectionism; judging other's motives; making goals and lists that you can't complete; mind reading; fantasy, codependent, rescuing; sleep problems, trouble concentrating, seeking/creating drama; gossip; using over-the-counter medication for pain, sleep or weight control; flirting.

....

Anxiety then leads to the inclusion of:

Speeding Up – **(Trying to outrun the anxiety which is usually the first sign of depression.)** Super busy and always in a hurry (finding good reason to justify the work); workaholic; can't relax; avoiding slowing down; feeling driven; can't turn off thoughts; skipping meals; binge eating (usually at night); overspending; can't identify own feelings/needs; repetitive negative thoughts; irritable; dramatic mood swings; too much caffeine; over exercising; nervousness; difficulty being alone and/or with people; difficulty listening to others; making excuses for having to "do it all."

....

Speeding Up then leads to the inclusion of:

Ticked Off – **(Getting adrenaline high on anger and aggression.)** Procrastination causing crisis in money, work, and relationships; increased sarcasm; black and white (all or nothing) thinking; feeling alone; nobody understands; overreacting, road rage; constant resentments; pushing others away; increasing isolation; blaming; arguing; irrational thinking; can't take criticism; defensive; people avoiding you; needing to be right; digestive problems; headaches; obsessive (stuck) thoughts; can't forgive; feeling superior; using intimidation.

....

Ticked Off then leads to the inclusion of:

Exhausted – **(Loss of physical and emotional energy; coming off the adrenaline high, and the onset of depression.)** Depressed; panicked; confused; hopelessness; sleeping too much or too little; can't cope; overwhelmed; crying for "no reason"; can't think; forgetful; pessimistic; helpless; tired; numb; wanting to run; constant cravings for old coping behaviors; thinking of using sex, drugs, or alcohol; seeking old unhealthy people & places; really isolating; people angry with you; self abuse; suicidal thoughts; spontaneous crying; no goals; survival mode; not returning phone calls; missing work; irritability; no appetite.

....

Exhausted then leads to the inclusion of:

Relapse – **(Returning to the place you swore you would never go again. Coping with life on your terms. You sitting in the driver's seat instead of God.)** Giving up and giving in; out of control; lost in your addiction; lying to yourself and others; feeling you just can't manage without your coping behaviors, at least for now. The result is the reinforcement of shame, guilt and condemnation; and feelings of abandonment and being alone.

....

PART TWO

Identify the most powerful behavior in each section and write it next to the corresponding heading.

Answer the following three questions:

1. How does it affect me? How do I feel in the moment?
2. How does it affect the important people in my life?
3. Why do I do this? What is the benefit for me?

Restoration: _____

1. _____
2. _____
3. _____

Forgetting Priorities: _____

1. _____
2. _____
3. _____

Anxiety: _____

1. _____
2. _____
3. _____

Speeding Up: _____

1. _____
2. _____
3. _____

Ticked Off: _____

1. _____
2. _____
3. _____

Exhausted: _____

1. _____
2. _____
3. _____

Relapse: _____

1. _____
2. _____
3. _____

GROUP CHECK-IN
COMPLETE 24 HOURS BEFORE GROUP

1. What is the lowest level you reached on the **FASTER Scale** this week?

_____

2. What was the **Double Bind** you were dealing with?

_____

_____

_____

_____

3. Where are you on your **Courageous Commitment to Change** from our last meeting?

_____

4. What information from your Betrayal & Beyond lesson was most applicable to your situation this week? What information had the most impact emotionally?

_____

_____

_____

5. What have you done to improve your relationship with your husband or other significant relationships this week?

_____

_____

_____

⊜ Lesson Two

UNHEALTHY ANGER

Thought for the week: *The first step toward healing is the diagnosis of the problem. If we are not aware of our blind spots, or our negative reactions, we will never be able to address them. We will continue to react when angered, instead of responding appropriately, with wisdom and insight, using skills we have developed along this journey.*

List five things you are thankful for this week.

1. _____
2. _____
3. _____
4. _____
5. _____

Write down the personal/prophetic promises God has shown you so far with the Scripture He has given you.

1. _____
   _____

2. _____
   _____

3. _____
   _____

4. _____
   _____

What did you feel after reading the letter, The Man I Thought I Married, to your group?

_____

_____

_____

_____

_____

_____

After taking the Anger Test, what emotions are you experiencing as you see the reality of your anger test results?

_____

_____

_____

_____

_____

_____

Write down which category of anger (Repressed Anger or Explosive Anger) you most identify with and share why.

_____

_____

_____

_____

_____

_____

COURAGEOUS COMMITMENT TO CHANGE

1. What area do you need to change or what challenge are you facing next week?

_____

_____

2. What will it cost you emotionally if you do change? What fear will you have to face?

_____

_____

3. What will it cost you if you don't change?

_____

_____

4. What is your plan to maintain your restoration regarding these changes?

_____

_____

5. Who will keep you accountable to this commitment?

Name _____ Day _____

Name _____ Day _____

Name _____ Day _____

6. What are the details of your accountability this week? What questions should they ask?

_____

_____

_____

FASTER SCALE

Adapted with permission from the *Genesis Process* by Michael Dye

PART ONE

Circle the behaviors on the FASTER Scale that you identify with in each section.

....

Restoration – (**Accepting life on God's terms, with trust, grace, mercy, vulnerability and gratitude**.) No current secrets; working to resolve problems; identifying fears and feelings; keeping commitments to meetings, prayer, family, church, people, goals, and self; being open and honest, making eye contact; increasing in relationships with God and others; true accountability.

....

Forgetting Priorities – (**Start believing the present circumstances and moving away from trusting God. Denial; flight; a change in what's important; how you spend your time, energy, and thoughts.**) Secrets; less time/energy for God, meetings, church; avoiding support and accountability people; superficial conversations; sarcasm; isolating; changes in goals; obsessed with relationships; breaking promises & commitments; neglecting family; preoccupation with material things, TV, computers, entertainment; procrastination; lying; overconfidence; bored; hiding money; image management; seeking to control situations and other people.

....

Forgetting Priorities will lead to the inclusion of:

Anxiety – (**A growing background noise of undefined fear; getting energy from emotions.**) Worry, using profanity, being fearful; being resentful; replaying old, negative thoughts; perfectionism; judging other's motives; making goals and lists that you can't complete; mind reading; fantasy, codependent, rescuing; sleep problems, trouble concentrating, seeking/creating drama; gossip; using over-the-counter medication for pain, sleep or weight control; flirting.

....

Anxiety then leads to the inclusion of:

Speeding Up – **(Trying to outrun the anxiety which is usually the first sign of depression.)** Super busy and always in a hurry (finding good reason to justify the work); workaholic; can't relax; avoiding slowing down; feeling driven; can't turn off thoughts; skipping meals; binge eating (usually at night); overspending; can't identify own feelings/needs; repetitive negative thoughts; irritable; dramatic mood swings; too much caffeine; over exercising; nervousness; difficulty being alone and/or with people; difficulty listening to others; making excuses for having to "do it all."

....

Speeding Up then leads to the inclusion of:

Ticked Off – **(Getting adrenaline high on anger and aggression.)** Procrastination causing crisis in money, work, and relationships; increased sarcasm; black and white (all or nothing) thinking; feeling alone; nobody understands; overreacting, road rage; constant resentments; pushing others away; increasing isolation; blaming; arguing; irrational thinking; can't take criticism; defensive; people avoiding you; needing to be right; digestive problems; headaches; obsessive (stuck) thoughts; can't forgive; feeling superior; using intimidation.

....

Ticked Off then leads to the inclusion of:

Exhausted – **(Loss of physical and emotional energy; coming off the adrenaline high, and the onset of depression.)** Depressed; panicked; confused; hopelessness; sleeping too much or too little; can't cope; overwhelmed; crying for "no reason"; can't think; forgetful; pessimistic; helpless; tired; numb; wanting to run; constant cravings for old coping behaviors; thinking of using sex, drugs, or alcohol; seeking old unhealthy people & places; really isolating; people angry with you; self abuse; suicidal thoughts; spontaneous crying; no goals; survival mode; not returning phone calls; missing work; irritability; no appetite.

....

Exhausted then leads to the inclusion of:

Relapse – **(Returning to the place you swore you would never go again. Coping with life on your terms. You sitting in the driver's seat instead of God.)** Giving up and giving in; out of control; lost in your addiction; lying to yourself and others; feeling you just can't manage without your coping behaviors, at least for now. The result is the reinforcement of shame, guilt and condemnation; and feelings of abandonment and being alone.

....

PART TWO

Identify the most powerful behavior in each section and write it next to the corresponding heading.

Answer the following three questions:
1. How does it affect me? How do I feel in the moment?
2. How does it affect the important people in my life?
3. Why do I do this? What is the benefit for me?

Restoration: _____

1. _____
2. _____
3. _____

Forgetting Priorities: _____

1. _____
2. _____
3. _____

Anxiety: _____

1. _____
2. _____
3. _____

Speeding Up: _____

1. _____
2. _____
3. _____

Ticked Off: _____

1. _____
2. _____
3. _____

Exhausted: _____

1. _____
2. _____
3. _____

Relapse: _____

1. _____
2. _____
3. _____

GROUP CHECK-IN
COMPLETE 24 HOURS BEFORE GROUP

1. What is the lowest level you reached on the **FASTER Scale** this week?

_____

2. What was the **Double Bind** you were dealing with?

_____

_____

_____

_____

3. Where are you on your **Courageous Commitment to Change** from our last meeting?

_____

4. What information from your Betrayal & Beyond lesson was most applicable to your situation this week? What information had the most impact emotionally?

_____

_____

_____

5. What have you done to improve your relationship with your husband or other significant relationships this week?

_____

_____

_____

⬚ *Lesson Three*
HEALTHY ANGER

Thought for the week: *Perhaps there have been times along this journey when you were not able to fully identify the emotions you were feeling. As you continue to learn to name your feelings, you will also continue to learn how to manage those feelings in healthy ways. Who knows? You may even discover a new hobby or gifting along the way.*

List five things you are thankful for this week.

1. _____
2. _____
3. _____
4. _____
5. _____

Write down the personal/prophetic promises God has shown you so far with the Scripture He has given you.

1. _____
   _____

2. _____
   _____

3. _____
   _____

4. _____
   _____

List another promise God might have given you during this process.

_____

_____

_____

Explain the picture you drew in your _Workbook_ about what comes to mind when you think of anger.

_____

_____

_____

_____

_____

_____

_____

When I was asked to write my story for the Betrayal & Beyond lesson, I took a notebook and pen, found a quiet, private place outside and began looking back over the past 25 years of my life with the man I loved. I began at the beginning, during our dating, and found myself writing page after page, hour after hour until I finally sat back in shock at what I had just discovered. There on paper was truth that "just one or two times with a prostitute" turned out to be years and years of betrayals that I had denied and lumped together in closed parts of my mind, pretending that only those "couple of times" had occurred. Now I looked at pages and pages; I'd been writing for six straight hours, non-stop. I held in my hand 25 years of reality and the dam called denial broke as the tears poured from the depths of my soul.

SHELBY

Like Shelby, it is important that you get out your anger. You may need more space than is provided for the following letter. If that is the case, write your letter on another piece of paper, holding back nothing. **Then, in the space allotted, write a summary of your original letter to read to your group.** It should be no more than a three minute read.

To The Man I Realize I Married:

_____

_____

_____

_____

_____

_____

_____

_____

_____

_____

_____

_____

_____

_____

_____

_____

_____

For your Commitment to Courageously Change this week you might want to do the following:

Practice using the Healthy Anger Cycle this week when opportunities present themselves. Give yourself the time to process these new skills and work them out.

- If needed, do a Double Bind to find out why you are angry and unable to process the event/situation further.

- Report back to your small group the progress you have experienced with a specific example. **Write your example here:**

_____

_____

_____

COURAGEOUS COMMITMENT TO CHANGE

1. What area do you need to change or what challenge are you facing next week?

_____

_____

2. What will it cost you emotionally if you do change? What fear will you have to face?

_____

_____

3. What will it cost you if you don't change?

_____

_____

4. What is your plan to maintain your restoration regarding these changes?

_____

_____

5. Who will keep you accountable to this commitment?

Name _____ Day _____

Name _____ Day _____

Name _____ Day _____

6. What are the details of your accountability this week? What questions should they ask?

_____

_____

_____

FASTER SCALE

Adapted with permission from the *Genesis Process* by Michael Dye

PART ONE

Circle the behaviors on the FASTER Scale that you identify with in each section.

....

Restoration – **(Accepting life on God's terms, with trust, grace, mercy, vulnerability and gratitude.)** No current secrets; working to resolve problems; identifying fears and feelings; keeping commitments to meetings, prayer, family, church, people, goals, and self; being open and honest, making eye contact; increasing in relationships with God and others; true accountability.

....

Forgetting Priorities – **(Start believing the present circumstances and moving away from trusting God. Denial; flight; a change in what's important; how you spend your time, energy, and thoughts.)** Secrets; less time/energy for God, meetings, church; avoiding support and accountability people; superficial conversations; sarcasm; isolating; changes in goals; obsessed with relationships; breaking promises & commitments; neglecting family; preoccupation with material things, TV, computers, entertainment; procrastination; lying; overconfidence; bored; hiding money; image management; seeking to control situations and other people.

....

Forgetting Priorities will lead to the inclusion of:

Anxiety – **(A growing background noise of undefined fear; getting energy from emotions.)** Worry, using profanity, being fearful; being resentful; replaying old, negative thoughts; perfectionism; judging other's motives; making goals and lists that you can't complete; mind reading; fantasy, codependent, rescuing; sleep problems, trouble concentrating, seeking/creating drama; gossip; using over-the-counter medication for pain, sleep or weight control; flirting.

....

Anxiety then leads to the inclusion of:

Speeding Up – **(Trying to outrun the anxiety which is usually the first sign of depression.)** Super busy and always in a hurry (finding good reason to justify the work); workaholic; can't relax; avoiding slowing down; feeling driven; can't turn off thoughts; skipping meals; binge eating (usually at night); overspending; can't identify own feelings/needs; repetitive negative thoughts; irritable; dramatic mood swings; too much caffeine; over exercising; nervousness; difficulty being alone and/or with people; difficulty listening to others; making excuses for having to "do it all."

....

Speeding Up then leads to the inclusion of:

Ticked Off – **(Getting adrenaline high on anger and aggression.)** Procrastination causing crisis in money, work, and relationships; increased sarcasm; black and white (all or nothing) thinking; feeling alone; nobody understands; overreacting, road rage; constant resentments; pushing others away; increasing isolation; blaming; arguing; irrational thinking; can't take criticism; defensive; people avoiding you; needing to be right; digestive problems; headaches; obsessive (stuck) thoughts; can't forgive; feeling superior; using intimidation.

....

Ticked Off then leads to the inclusion of:

Exhausted – **(Loss of physical and emotional energy; coming off the adrenaline high, and the onset of depression.)** Depressed; panicked; confused; hopelessness; sleeping too much or too little; can't cope; overwhelmed; crying for "no reason"; can't think; forgetful; pessimistic; helpless; tired; numb; wanting to run; constant cravings for old coping behaviors; thinking of using sex, drugs, or alcohol; seeking old unhealthy people & places; really isolating; people angry with you; self abuse; suicidal thoughts; spontaneous crying; no goals; survival mode; not returning phone calls; missing work; irritability; no appetite.

....

Exhausted then leads to the inclusion of:

Relapse – **(Returning to the place you swore you would never go again. Coping with life on your terms. You sitting in the driver's seat instead of God.)** Giving up and giving in; out of control; lost in your addiction; lying to yourself and others; feeling you just can't manage without your coping behaviors, at least for now. The result is the reinforcement of shame, guilt and condemnation; and feelings of abandonment and being alone.

....

PART TWO

Identify the most powerful behavior in each section and write it next to the corresponding heading.

Answer the following three questions:

1. How does it affect me? How do I feel in the moment?
2. How does it affect the important people in my life?
3. Why do I do this? What is the benefit for me?

Restoration: _____

1. _____
2. _____
3. _____

Forgetting Priorities: _____

1. _____
2. _____
3. _____

Anxiety: _____

1. _____
2. _____
3. _____

Speeding Up: _____

1. _____
2. _____
3. _____

Ticked Off: _____

1. _____
2. _____
3. _____

Exhausted: _____

1. _____
2. _____
3. _____

Relapse: _____

1. _____
2. _____
3. _____

GROUP CHECK-IN
COMPLETE 24 HOURS BEFORE GROUP

1. What is the lowest level you reached on the **FASTER Scale** this week?

_____

2. What was the **Double Bind** you were dealing with?

_____

_____

_____

_____

3. Where are you on your **Courageous Commitment to Change** from our last meeting?

_____

4. What information from your Betrayal & Beyond lesson was most applicable to your situation this week? What information had the most impact emotionally?

_____

_____

_____

5. What have you done to improve your relationship with your husband or other significant relationships this week?

_____

_____

_____

⬛ Lesson Four

GRIEVING YOUR LOSSES

Thought for the week: Through this journey, you may find that some long-held friendships are being weeded away, and you may feel as if you are standing alone in your life's garden. But then, as you allow God to nurture you through this time, you will see new growth begin to develop. New friends, new sisters, who understand and who share your journey will come alongside you in this new season of your life. God weeds our garden to prepare for the beautiful flowers to come.

List five things you are thankful for this week.

1. _____
2. _____
3. _____
4. _____
5. _____

Write down the personal/prophetic promises God has shown you so far with the Scripture He has given you.

1. _____
2. _____
3. _____
4. _____
5. _____

How did you feel writing your letter, "To the Man I Realize I Married," with all the reality that entailed?

_____

_____

_____

_____

_____

_____

As you wrote that letter, what were you saying goodbye to? (i.e. looking like the "perfect family," financial stability—at least for now…)

_____

_____

_____

_____

_____

_____

How did you feel as you read it to your group?

_____

_____

_____

_____

_____

_____

Meditate on this Scripture and then share the positive things you see God doing even in the midst of your pain.

> *You turned my wailing into dancing; you removed my sackcloth*
> *and clothed me with joy, that my heart may sing to you and not be silent.*
> *LORD my God, I will praise you forever.*
> PSALM 30:11-12 (NIV)

_____

_____

_____

_____

_____

In light of that Scripture and the raw material chart you filled out, what could you expect God to do in the future?

_____

_____

_____

_____

_____

The leader of your small group might have you do something physical to grieve and release the losses. But keep in mind that, at any time, you might want to go back to the four suggestions at the end of Chapter 7, Lesson 4 of your *Workbook* and do something physical to give those losses to the Lord. **List one of the four you could commit to do in the future:**

_____

_____

_____

COURAGEOUS COMMITMENT TO CHANGE

1. What area do you need to change or what challenge are you facing next week?

_____

_____

2. What will it cost you emotionally if you do change? What fear will you have to face?

_____

_____

3. What will it cost you if you don't change?

_____

_____

4. What is your plan to maintain your restoration regarding these changes?

_____

_____

5. Who will keep you accountable to this commitment?

Name _____ Day _____

Name _____ Day _____

Name _____ Day _____

6. What are the details of your accountability this week? What questions should they ask?

_____

_____

_____

FASTER SCALE

Adapted with permission from the *Genesis Process* by Michael Dye

PART ONE

Circle the behaviors on the FASTER Scale that you identify with in each section.

....

Restoration – (**Accepting life on God's terms, with trust, grace, mercy, vulnerability and gratitude**.) No current secrets; working to resolve problems; identifying fears and feelings; keeping commitments to meetings, prayer, family, church, people, goals, and self; being open and honest, making eye contact; increasing in relationships with God and others; true accountability.

....

Forgetting Priorities – (**Start believing the present circumstances and moving away from trusting God. Denial; flight; a change in what's important; how you spend your time, energy, and thoughts.**) Secrets; less time/energy for God, meetings, church; avoiding support and accountability people; superficial conversations; sarcasm; isolating; changes in goals; obsessed with relationships; breaking promises & commitments; neglecting family; preoccupation with material things, TV, computers, entertainment; procrastination; lying; overconfidence; bored; hiding money; image management; seeking to control situations and other people.

....

Forgetting Priorities will lead to the inclusion of:

Anxiety – (**A growing background noise of undefined fear; getting energy from emotions.**) Worry, using profanity, being fearful; being resentful; replaying old, negative thoughts; perfectionism; judging other's motives; making goals and lists that you can't complete; mind reading; fantasy, codependent, rescuing; sleep problems, trouble concentrating, seeking/creating drama; gossip; using over-the-counter medication for pain, sleep or weight control; flirting.

....

Anxiety then leads to the inclusion of:

Speeding Up – **(Trying to outrun the anxiety which is usually the first sign of depression.)** Super busy and always in a hurry (finding good reason to justify the work); workaholic; can't relax; avoiding slowing down; feeling driven; can't turn off thoughts; skipping meals; binge eating (usually at night); overspending; can't identify own feelings/needs; repetitive negative thoughts; irritable; dramatic mood swings; too much caffeine; over exercising; nervousness; difficulty being alone and/or with people; difficulty listening to others; making excuses for having to "do it all."

....

Speeding Up then leads to the inclusion of:

Ticked Off – **(Getting adrenaline high on anger and aggression.)** Procrastination causing crisis in money, work, and relationships; increased sarcasm; black and white (all or nothing) thinking; feeling alone; nobody understands; overreacting, road rage; constant resentments; pushing others away; increasing isolation; blaming; arguing; irrational thinking; can't take criticism; defensive; people avoiding you; needing to be right; digestive problems; headaches; obsessive (stuck) thoughts; can't forgive; feeling superior; using intimidation.

....

Ticked Off then leads to the inclusion of:

Exhausted – **(Loss of physical and emotional energy; coming off the adrenaline high, and the onset of depression.)** Depressed; panicked; confused; hopelessness; sleeping too much or too little; can't cope; overwhelmed; crying for "no reason"; can't think; forgetful; pessimistic; helpless; tired; numb; wanting to run; constant cravings for old coping behaviors; thinking of using sex, drugs, or alcohol; seeking old unhealthy people & places; really isolating; people angry with you; self abuse; suicidal thoughts; spontaneous crying; no goals; survival mode; not returning phone calls; missing work; irritability; no appetite.

....

Exhausted then leads to the inclusion of:

Relapse – **(Returning to the place you swore you would never go again. Coping with life on your terms. You sitting in the driver's seat instead of God.)** Giving up and giving in; out of control; lost in your addiction; lying to yourself and others; feeling you just can't manage without your coping behaviors, at least for now. The result is the reinforcement of shame, guilt and condemnation; and feelings of abandonment and being alone.

....

PART TWO

Identify the most powerful behavior in each section and write it next to the corresponding heading.

Answer the following three questions:
1. How does it affect me? How do I feel in the moment?
2. How does it affect the important people in my life?
3. Why do I do this? What is the benefit for me?

Restoration: _____

1. _____
2. _____
3. _____

Forgetting Priorities: _____

1. _____
2. _____
3. _____

Anxiety: _____

1. _____
2. _____
3. _____

Speeding Up: _____

1. _____
2. _____
3. _____

Ticked Off: _____

1. _____
2. _____
3. _____

Exhausted: _____

1. _____
2. _____
3. _____

Relapse: _____

1. _____
2. _____
3. _____

GROUP CHECK-IN
COMPLETE 24 HOURS BEFORE GROUP

1. What is the lowest level you reached on the **FASTER Scale** this week?

_____

2. What was the **Double Bind** you were dealing with?

_____

_____

_____

_____

3. Where are you on your **Courageous Commitment to Change** from our last meeting?

_____

4. What information from your Betrayal & Beyond lesson was most applicable to your situation this week? What information had the most impact emotionally?

_____

_____

_____

5. What have you done to improve your relationship with your husband or other significant relationships this week?

_____

_____

_____

Chapter Eight

HEALING AND FORGIVENESS

⬦ *Lesson One*

WHAT IS FORGIVENESS?

Thought for the week: *There is no doubt that along this courageous journey you have experienced great pain at the hands of another, or of many others. While this pain was never God's plan for you, He is uniquely able to turn your mourning into dancing as you allow Him to walk with you.*

List five things you are thankful for this week.

1. _____
2. _____
3. _____
4. _____
5. _____

Write down the personal/prophetic promises God has shown you so far with the Scripture He has given you.

1. _____
2. _____
3. _____
4. _____
5. _____

From your group last week you were asked to write down losses from lesson one and your raw material list on sticky notes. If there were some you were not ready to lay at the foot of the cross, use the following space to write out more of the hurt associated with each loss and ask God for His help in letting go of that loss.

_____

_____

_____

_____

_____

_____

_____

Which of the six myths have you believed were forgiveness? Journal how believing these affected you.

_____

_____

_____

_____

_____

On the chart provided on the following page, identify specific people who hurt or victimized you in your past and write out how they hurt you. (Look back to your Personal Timeline if needed.) In the fourth column, consider how you would feel if you were to see them today. Are there still negative feelings, fears, or other strong reactions? List those responses. Finally, consider whether you have any guilt or blame for your part in those painful times of your past. If you feel a sense of shame or guilt, place a check mark in the final column. (For example, it is very common for survivors of childhood sexual abuse to have guilt, or for the wife of a sex addict to take on shame regarding her husband's behaviors or consequences.)

IDENTIFYING MY PAST HURTS

PERSON WHO HURT ME	DESCRIPTION OF THE HURT	CURRENT RELATIONSHIP	FEELINGS (See Feelings Wheel in *Workbook* appendix)	GUILT/ SHAME
Example: My Mom	She was controlling and codependent to my dad's drinking.	I have only seen her occasionally, but try to keep my distance. She is still bitter and tries to control me.	Still hurt, angry, and bitter towards her. Prefer to have nothing to do with her.	

PERSON WHO HURT ME	DESCRIPTION OF THE HURT	CURRENT RELATIONSHIP	FEELINGS (See Feelings Wheel in *Workbook* appendix)	GUILT/ SHAME

Take time to write a letter to each person on your list. State the hurt that was created by their actions and the emotions you have felt as a result. Allow your anger to be expressed. One person shared, "As I wrote, I felt all the anger in my heart flowing out, down my arm, and through the pen I used to write the letter." Remember, Scripture says be angry, but do not sin. In other words, express your anger in a way that will bring health to you.

The letters are for your healing, and may or may not be sent. We recommend that you finish this chapter and all the lessons before making any decisions about whether or not to send your letters. It is good to come to a place where you are able to forgive them no matter what their response to your letter might be. Consult with your group, counselor or pastor before sending a letter. After finishing each letter, write a prayer, sharing with God your feelings about forgiving this person.

THE NEXT EIGHT PAGES ARE SET ASIDE FOR THESE LETTERS:

Dear _____

_____

_____

_____

_____

_____

_____

_____

_____

_____

_____

_____

_____

_____

_____

_____

_____

_____

_____

_____

_____

_____

_____

_____

_____

_____

Dear _____

Dear _____

Dear _____

COURAGEOUS COMMITMENT TO CHANGE

1. What area do you need to change or what challenge are you facing next week?

_____

_____

2. What will it cost you emotionally if you do change? What fear will you have to face?

_____

_____

3. What will it cost you if you don't change?

_____

_____

4. What is your plan to maintain your restoration regarding these changes?

_____

_____

5. Who will keep you accountable to this commitment?

Name _____   Day _____

Name _____   Day _____

Name _____   Day _____

6. What are the details of your accountability this week? What questions should they ask?

_____

_____

_____

FASTER SCALE

Adapted with permission from the *Genesis Process* by Michael Dye

PART ONE

Circle the behaviors on the FASTER Scale that you identify with in each section.

....

Restoration – (**Accepting life on God's terms, with trust, grace, mercy, vulnerability and gratitude.**) No current secrets; working to resolve problems; identifying fears and feelings; keeping commitments to meetings, prayer, family, church, people, goals, and self; being open and honest, making eye contact; increasing in relationships with God and others; true accountability.

....

Forgetting Priorities – (**Start believing the present circumstances and moving away from trusting God. Denial; flight; a change in what's important; how you spend your time, energy, and thoughts.**) Secrets; less time/energy for God, meetings, church; avoiding support and accountability people; superficial conversations; sarcasm; isolating; changes in goals; obsessed with relationships; breaking promises & commitments; neglecting family; preoccupation with material things, TV, computers, entertainment; procrastination; lying; overconfidence; bored; hiding money; image management; seeking to control situations and other people.

....

Forgetting Priorities will lead to the inclusion of:

Anxiety – (**A growing background noise of undefined fear; getting energy from emotions.**) Worry, using profanity, being fearful; being resentful; replaying old, negative thoughts; perfectionism; judging other's motives; making goals and lists that you can't complete; mind reading; fantasy, codependent, rescuing; sleep problems, trouble concentrating, seeking/creating drama; gossip; using over-the-counter medication for pain, sleep or weight control; flirting.

....

Anxiety then leads to the inclusion of:

Speeding Up – (Trying to outrun the anxiety which is usually the first sign of depression.) Super busy and always in a hurry (finding good reason to justify the work); workaholic; can't relax; avoiding slowing down; feeling driven; can't turn off thoughts; skipping meals; binge eating (usually at night); overspending; can't identify own feelings/needs; repetitive negative thoughts; irritable; dramatic mood swings; too much caffeine; over exercising; nervousness; difficulty being alone and/or with people; difficulty listening to others; making excuses for having to "do it all."

....

Speeding Up then leads to the inclusion of:

Ticked Off – (Getting adrenaline high on anger and aggression.) Procrastination causing crisis in money, work, and relationships; increased sarcasm; black and white (all or nothing) thinking; feeling alone; nobody understands; overreacting, road rage; constant resentments; pushing others away; increasing isolation; blaming; arguing; irrational thinking; can't take criticism; defensive; people avoiding you; needing to be right; digestive problems; headaches; obsessive (stuck) thoughts; can't forgive; feeling superior; using intimidation.

....

Ticked Off then leads to the inclusion of:

Exhausted – (Loss of physical and emotional energy; coming off the adrenaline high, and the onset of depression.) Depressed; panicked; confused; hopelessness; sleeping too much or too little; can't cope; overwhelmed; crying for "no reason"; can't think; forgetful; pessimistic; helpless; tired; numb; wanting to run; constant cravings for old coping behaviors; thinking of using sex, drugs, or alcohol; seeking old unhealthy people & places; really isolating; people angry with you; self abuse; suicidal thoughts; spontaneous crying; no goals; survival mode; not returning phone calls; missing work; irritability; no appetite.

....

Exhausted then leads to the inclusion of:

Relapse – (Returning to the place you swore you would never go again. Coping with life on your terms. You sitting in the driver's seat instead of God.) Giving up and giving in; out of control; lost in your addiction; lying to yourself and others; feeling you just can't manage without your coping behaviors, at least for now. The result is the reinforcement of shame, guilt and condemnation; and feelings of abandonment and being alone.

....

194

PART TWO

Identify the most powerful behavior in each section and write it next to the corresponding heading.

Answer the following three questions:
  1. How does it affect me? How do I feel in the moment?
  2. How does it affect the important people in my life?
  3. Why do I do this? What is the benefit for me?

Restoration: _____
1. _____
2. _____
3. _____

Forgetting Priorities: _____
1. _____
2. _____
3. _____

Anxiety: _____
1. _____
2. _____
3. _____

Speeding Up: _____
1. _____
2. _____
3. _____

Ticked Off: _____
1. _____
2. _____
3. _____

Exhausted: _____
1. _____
2. _____
3. _____

Relapse: _____
1. _____
2. _____
3. _____

GROUP CHECK-IN
COMPLETE 24 HOURS BEFORE GROUP

1. What is the lowest level you reached on the **FASTER Scale** this week?

_____

2. What was the **Double Bind** you were dealing with?

_____

_____

_____

_____

3. Where are you on your **Courageous Commitment to Change** from our last meeting?

_____

4. What information from your Betrayal & Beyond lesson was most applicable to your situation this week? What information had the most impact emotionally?

_____

_____

_____

5. What have you done to improve your relationship with your husband or other significant relationships this week?

_____

_____

_____

⬚ 𝓛𝓮𝓼𝓼𝓸𝓷 𝓣𝔀𝓸
WHY SHOULD I FORGIVE?

Thought for the week: *Forgiveness is a difficult process; it is not easy. A heroine does not take the easy way out. You are a heroine. Continue on your courageous journey.*

List five things you are thankful for this week.

1. _____
2. _____
3. _____
4. _____
5. _____

Write down the personal/prophetic promises God has shown you so far with the Scripture He has given you.

1. _____
2. _____
3. _____
4. _____
5. _____

Discuss your feelings about sharing from the list of people who have hurt you from your last lesson.

_____

_____

_____

_____

_____

_____

Share what this statement from your _Workbook_ lesson means to you:

I forgave to set a prisoner free, only to discover that the prisoner was me.
AUTHOR UNKNOWN

_____

_____

_____

_____

_____

Look through the Scriptures on forgiveness from Chapter 8, Lessons 1-2 of your _Workbook_. Share the Scriptures that meant the most to you and why.

_____

_____

_____

_____

_____

Summarize the benefits to forgiving, according to Scripture.

_____

_____

_____

_____

_____

What would be the biggest benefit or blessing to you if you could totally forgive?

_____

_____

_____

_____

_____

What experience in your past has shown these benefits to be true?

_____

_____

_____

_____

_____

From God's perspective, why do you think He wants us to have a forgiving spirit?

_____

_____

_____

Share in your own words how unforgiveness can affect us physically, according to Dr. Michael Barry.

_____

_____

_____

_____

_____

_____

In light of what you have learned from Scripture, go back through your list of People Who Have Hurt Me. Find one person to whom you can allow God to apply these Scriptures. Journal your feelings about forgiving them. You might even want to do a Double Bind exercise on why it is so difficult. _(Example: If I don't forgive, bitterness will continue to grow in my heart…If I do forgive and write a letter, the person might blow me off and deny or make light of my hurt.)_

_____

_____

_____

_____

_____

_____

_____

_____

_____

_____

COURAGEOUS COMMITMENT TO CHANGE

1. What area do you need to change or what challenge are you facing next week?

_____

_____

2. What will it cost you emotionally if you do change? What fear will you have to face?

_____

_____

3. What will it cost you if you don't change?

_____

_____

4. What is your plan to maintain your restoration regarding these changes?

_____

_____

5. Who will keep you accountable to this commitment?

Name _____ Day _____

Name _____ Day _____

Name _____ Day _____

6. What are the details of your accountability this week? What questions should they ask?

_____

_____

_____

FASTER SCALE

Adapted with permission from the *Genesis Process* by Michael Dye

PART ONE

Circle the behaviors on the FASTER Scale that you identify with in each section.

....

Restoration – (**Accepting life on God's terms, with trust, grace, mercy, vulnerability and gratitude**.) No current secrets; working to resolve problems; identifying fears and feelings; keeping commitments to meetings, prayer, family, church, people, goals, and self; being open and honest, making eye contact; increasing in relationships with God and others; true accountability.

....

Forgetting Priorities – (**Start believing the present circumstances and moving away from trusting God. Denial; flight; a change in what's important; how you spend your time, energy, and thoughts.**) Secrets; less time/energy for God, meetings, church; avoiding support and accountability people; superficial conversations; sarcasm; isolating; changes in goals; obsessed with relationships; breaking promises & commitments; neglecting family; preoccupation with material things, TV, computers, entertainment; procrastination; lying; overconfidence; bored; hiding money; image management; seeking to control situations and other people.

....

Forgetting Priorities will lead to the inclusion of:

Anxiety – (**A growing background noise of undefined fear; getting energy from emotions.**) Worry, using profanity, being fearful; being resentful; replaying old, negative thoughts; perfectionism; judging other's motives; making goals and lists that you can't complete; mind reading; fantasy, codependent, rescuing; sleep problems, trouble concentrating, seeking/creating drama; gossip; using over-the-counter medication for pain, sleep or weight control; flirting.

....

Anxiety then leads to the inclusion of:

Speeding Up – **(Trying to outrun the anxiety which is usually the first sign of depression.)** Super busy and always in a hurry (finding good reason to justify the work); workaholic; can't relax; avoiding slowing down; feeling driven; can't turn off thoughts; skipping meals; binge eating (usually at night); overspending; can't identify own feelings/needs; repetitive negative thoughts; irritable; dramatic mood swings; too much caffeine; over exercising; nervousness; difficulty being alone and/or with people; difficulty listening to others; making excuses for having to "do it all."

....

Speeding Up then leads to the inclusion of:

Ticked Off – **(Getting adrenaline high on anger and aggression.)** Procrastination causing crisis in money, work, and relationships; increased sarcasm; black and white (all or nothing) thinking; feeling alone; nobody understands; overreacting, road rage; constant resentments; pushing others away; increasing isolation; blaming; arguing; irrational thinking; can't take criticism; defensive; people avoiding you; needing to be right; digestive problems; headaches; obsessive (stuck) thoughts; can't forgive; feeling superior; using intimidation.

....

Ticked Off then leads to the inclusion of:

Exhausted – **(Loss of physical and emotional energy; coming off the adrenaline high, and the onset of depression.)** Depressed; panicked; confused; hopelessness; sleeping too much or too little; can't cope; overwhelmed; crying for "no reason"; can't think; forgetful; pessimistic; helpless; tired; numb; wanting to run; constant cravings for old coping behaviors; thinking of using sex, drugs, or alcohol; seeking old unhealthy people & places; really isolating; people angry with you; self abuse; suicidal thoughts; spontaneous crying; no goals; survival mode; not returning phone calls; missing work; irritability; no appetite.

....

Exhausted then leads to the inclusion of:

Relapse – **(Returning to the place you swore you would never go again. Coping with life on your terms. You sitting in the driver's seat instead of God.)** Giving up and giving in; out of control; lost in your addiction; lying to yourself and others; feeling you just can't manage without your coping behaviors, at least for now. The result is the reinforcement of shame, guilt and condemnation; and feelings of abandonment and being alone.

....

PART TWO

Identify the most powerful behavior in each section and write it next to the corresponding heading.

Answer the following three questions:
1. How does it affect me? How do I feel in the moment?
2. How does it affect the important people in my life?
3. Why do I do this? What is the benefit for me?

Restoration: _____
1. _____
2. _____
3. _____

Forgetting Priorities: _____
1. _____
2. _____
3. _____

Anxiety: _____
1. _____
2. _____
3. _____

Speeding Up: _____
1. _____
2. _____
3. _____

Ticked Off: _____
1. _____
2. _____
3. _____

Exhausted: _____
1. _____
2. _____
3. _____

Relapse: _____
1. _____
2. _____
3. _____

GROUP CHECK-IN
COMPLETE 24 HOURS BEFORE GROUP

1. What is the lowest level you reached on the **FASTER Scale** this week?

_____

2. What was the **Double Bind** you were dealing with?

_____

_____

_____

_____

3. Where are you on your **Courageous Commitment to Change** from our last meeting?

_____

4. What information from your Betrayal & Beyond lesson was most applicable to your situation this week? What information had the most impact emotionally?

_____

_____

_____

5. What have you done to improve your relationship with your husband or other significant relationships this week?

_____

_____

_____

📄 Lesson Three

WHOM DO I FORGIVE?

Thought for the week: *Forgiving those who have wronged us can be painful. But nothing is as painful as allowing bitterness to come between you and the blessing God has for you at the end of your journey.*

List five things you are thankful for this week.

1. _____
2. _____
3. _____
4. _____
5. _____

Write down the personal/prophetic promises God has shown you so far with the Scripture He has given you.

1. _____
2. _____
3. _____
4. _____
5. _____

Journal in depth about the root causes and why you may be holding some judgments and vows. Remember, judgments put people in a place where you don't have to trust them. How might that apply to your root causes?

_____

_____

_____

_____

_____

_____

_____

_____

_____

_____

_____

_____

_____

What does this Scripture mean to you?

> *"Do not judge, or you too will be judged. For in the same way you judge others, you will be judged, and with the measure you use, it will be measured to you."*
>
> MATTHEW 7:1-2 (NIV)

_____

_____

_____

_____

_____

As you look at the charts you filled out in this lesson's *Workbook*, ask God whether there are any vows you have made regarding the people that you listed.

Look back at the list of judgments and vows that were true for you. They can become self-curses, or self-fulfilling prophecies: The lies you've told yourself to survive. "Whatever I do, I won't be enough." "All men/women are _____."

List those you realize you have been carrying:

_____
_____
_____
_____
_____
_____
_____
_____
_____
_____
_____
_____
_____
_____
_____

For every vow or judgment you have made, pray this prayer:

Lord forgive me for speaking this vow/judgment _____. I realize I made that vow/judgment out of fear to protect myself and survive. You said you have inscribed my name in the palms of your hands and you would not forget me (Isaiah 49:15-16). So rather than live in fear and trust this vow, today I choose to trust You to protect me.

Meditate on these Scriptures from Isaiah and Psalm. Then write down what they each mean to you in light of the prayers you have just prayed:

> *Can a woman forget her nursing child, and not have compassion on the son (daughter) of her womb? Surely they may forget, yet I will not forget you. See, I have inscribed you on the palms of My hands...*
>
> ISAIAH 49:15-16 (NKJV)

_____

_____

_____

_____

_____

> *You have also given me the shield of Your salvation; Your right hand has held me up, your gentleness has made me great. You enlarge my path under me, so my feet did not slip.*
>
> PSALM 18:35-36 (NKJV)

_____

_____

_____

_____

_____

Forgive and bless: You will know that you have fully forgiven someone when you can pray and ask God to bless him or her. You may never have any contact with that person again because they are not safe for you, but you can, with peace in your heart, pray blessing on their life.

It may take time and you may need to come back to this lesson, but at some point if you can come to a place where you say,

"God bless _____ (put his/her name here) **with Your abundant mercies."**

Then you know real healing has taken place.

Powerful. Profound. In this one simple statement your attitude, feelings and heart turn from anger, frustration and resentment to peace, safety and trust in the One who can take care of every problem. Try it. It even works for people you don't know personally, like those drivers who cut you off on the highway!

Finally go back and review the two lists of people you need to forgive and try this test for forgiveness: Say, "God bless _____ **with Your abundant mercies."**

1. Allow yourself to listen to your heart response. If you sense peace go on to the next name on the list.

2. If you did not sense peace add a check mark into the "not yet" column. There are most likely more layers to look at regarding this person.

3. After you finish, journal about your experience.

_____

_____

_____

_____

_____

_____

_____

_____

_____

_____

_____

_____

_____

_____

_____

Describe your response to the idea that you could be mad or bitter towards God.

_____

_____

_____

_____

_____

_____

_____

_____

In light of what God spoke to Erica in her dream, what might He be saying to you personally? If nothing immediately comes to mind, ask God to speak to you in terms that would help you to understand how He sees you and how His hand might have been at work in your life.

_____

_____

_____

_____

_____

_____

_____

_____

_____

COURAGEOUS COMMITMENT TO CHANGE

1. What area do you need to change or what challenge are you facing next week?

_____

_____

2. What will it cost you emotionally if you do change? What fear will you have to face?

_____

_____

3. What will it cost you if you don't change?

_____

_____

4. What is your plan to maintain your restoration regarding these changes?

_____

_____

5. Who will keep you accountable to this commitment?

Name _____   Day _____

Name _____   Day _____

Name _____   Day _____

6. What are the details of your accountability this week? What questions should they ask?

_____

_____

_____

FASTER SCALE

Adapted with permission from the *Genesis Process* by Michael Dye

PART ONE

Circle the behaviors on the FASTER Scale that you identify with in each section.

....

Restoration – **(Accepting life on God's terms, with trust, grace, mercy, vulnerability and gratitude.**) No current secrets; working to resolve problems; identifying fears and feelings; keeping commitments to meetings, prayer, family, church, people, goals, and self; being open and honest, making eye contact; increasing in relationships with God and others; true accountability.

....

Forgetting Priorities – **(Start believing the present circumstances and moving away from trusting God. Denial; flight; a change in what's important; how you spend your time, energy, and thoughts.**) Secrets; less time/energy for God, meetings, church; avoiding support and accountability people; superficial conversations; sarcasm; isolating; changes in goals; obsessed with relationships; breaking promises & commitments; neglecting family; preoccupation with material things, TV, computers, entertainment; procrastination; lying; overconfidence; bored; hiding money; image management; seeking to control situations and other people.

....

Forgetting Priorities will lead to the inclusion of:

Anxiety – **(A growing background noise of undefined fear; getting energy from emotions.**) Worry, using profanity, being fearful; being resentful; replaying old, negative thoughts; perfectionism; judging other's motives; making goals and lists that you can't complete; mind reading; fantasy, codependent, rescuing; sleep problems, trouble concentrating, seeking/creating drama; gossip; using over-the-counter medication for pain, sleep or weight control; flirting.

....

213

Anxiety then leads to the inclusion of:

Speeding Up – (Trying to outrun the anxiety which is usually the first sign of depression.) Super busy and always in a hurry (finding good reason to justify the work); workaholic; can't relax; avoiding slowing down; feeling driven; can't turn off thoughts; skipping meals; binge eating (usually at night); overspending; can't identify own feelings/needs; repetitive negative thoughts; irritable; dramatic mood swings; too much caffeine; over exercising; nervousness; difficulty being alone and/or with people; difficulty listening to others; making excuses for having to "do it all."

....

Speeding Up then leads to the inclusion of:

Ticked Off – (Getting adrenaline high on anger and aggression.) Procrastination causing crisis in money, work, and relationships; increased sarcasm; black and white (all or nothing) thinking; feeling alone; nobody understands; overreacting, road rage; constant resentments; pushing others away; increasing isolation; blaming; arguing; irrational thinking; can't take criticism; defensive; people avoiding you; needing to be right; digestive problems; headaches; obsessive (stuck) thoughts; can't forgive; feeling superior; using intimidation.

....

Ticked Off then leads to the inclusion of:

Exhausted – (Loss of physical and emotional energy; coming off the adrenaline high, and the onset of depression.) Depressed; panicked; confused; hopelessness; sleeping too much or too little; can't cope; overwhelmed; crying for "no reason"; can't think; forgetful; pessimistic; helpless; tired; numb; wanting to run; constant cravings for old coping behaviors; thinking of using sex, drugs, or alcohol; seeking old unhealthy people & places; really isolating; people angry with you; self abuse; suicidal thoughts; spontaneous crying; no goals; survival mode; not returning phone calls; missing work; irritability; no appetite.

....

Exhausted then leads to the inclusion of:

Relapse – (Returning to the place you swore you would never go again. Coping with life on your terms. You sitting in the driver's seat instead of God.) Giving up and giving in; out of control; lost in your addiction; lying to yourself and others; feeling you just can't manage without your coping behaviors, at least for now. The result is the reinforcement of shame, guilt and condemnation; and feelings of abandonment and being alone.

....

PART TWO

Identify the most powerful behavior in each section and write it next to the corresponding heading.

Answer the following three questions:
1. How does it affect me? How do I feel in the moment?
2. How does it affect the important people in my life?
3. Why do I do this? What is the benefit for me?

Restoration: _____
1. _____
2. _____
3. _____

Forgetting Priorities: _____
1. _____
2. _____
3. _____

Anxiety: _____
1. _____
2. _____
3. _____

Speeding Up: _____
1. _____
2. _____
3. _____

Ticked Off: _____
1. _____
2. _____
3. _____

Exhausted: _____
1. _____
2. _____
3. _____

Relapse: _____
1. _____
2. _____
3. _____

GROUP CHECK-IN
COMPLETE 24 HOURS BEFORE GROUP

1. What is the lowest level you reached on the **FASTER Scale** this week?

_____

2. What was the **Double Bind** you were dealing with?

_____

_____

_____

_____

3. Where are you on your **Courageous Commitment to Change** from our last meeting?

_____

4. What information from your Betrayal & Beyond lesson was most applicable to your situation this week? What information had the most impact emotionally?

_____

_____

_____

5. What have you done to improve your relationship with your husband or other significant relationships this week?

_____

_____

_____

ⓔ Lesson Four

HOW DO I FORGIVE?

Thought for the week: *A heroine understands that there is a difference between forgiveness and reconciliation. She can choose to forgive, even when reconciliation may not be possible.*

List five things you are thankful for this week.

1. _____
2. _____
3. _____
4. _____
5. _____

Write down the personal/prophetic promises God has shown you so far with the Scripture He has given you.

1. _____
2. _____
3. _____
4. _____
5. _____

The first step towards forgiveness in your *Workbook* was to forgive God. In last week's journaling you began to ponder your anger toward God. Now take the time to confess your frustration, anger or blame to God. Be completely honest with Him. Write your prayer here.

_____

_____

_____

_____

_____

_____

_____

Proxy Exercise: Using a proxy, or a stand-in, to help you forgive can also seal your choice to forgive.

To work towards forgiveness, your group leader may pair you up to do the following exercise:

- First, pray with the proxy and ask the Lord to give you eyes to see the one you need to forgive, and to give the proxy God's heart for your offender. Then, the proxy looks at you and asks, "How have I hurt you?" The proxy listens, never interrupting, never trying to explain or excuse; they just listen.

- Next, you pour out all you wish you could say until you are silent for a bit. The proxy then recaps some of your words: "It hurt you when I _____. How else have I hurt you?"

- The proxy allows silence and just listens again. The proxy continues to listen and reflect until you answer, "No, I think that is all."

- The proxy sums up what you have said one last time and then says, "_____ (your name), I don't deserve forgiveness because I hurt you so badly when I _____ *[name a few of the offenses]*, but I want to ask if you will forgive me."

This is a powerful way to get release and experience the freedom that forgiveness can bring. It is also a wonderful tool to use when the person you need to forgive is not safe or is no longer living.

SOUL-TIES

As you prayed to renounce any soul-ties and/or judgments and vows from previous lessons, write a prayer thanking God for His power to deliver and release you from previous obstacles that would keep you stuck in unforgiveness.

_____

_____

_____

_____

_____

_____

_____

_____

Out of the freedom that comes from forgiveness, you will be able to hear God as never before. Spend some time listening to what He would say, expecting the Holy Spirit to speak to you. Journal below as words come.

_____

_____

_____

_____

_____

_____

_____

_____

LETTING GO

The next step toward health is recognizing that you can only change yourself, not the other person. By letting go we release that person to God, and by letting go we allow natural consequences to be the teacher. The following anonymous poem has been printed in many newspapers and in recovery literature. This poem will help you begin to recognize and remove the planks you may have in our own eyes, as referred to in Matthew 7.

LETTING GO TAKES LOVE

To "let go" does not mean to stop caring;
it means I can't do it for someone else.

To "let go" is not to cut myself off;
it is the realization that I can't control another.

To "let go" is not to enable, but
to allow learning from natural consequences.

To "let go" is to admit powerlessness,
which means the outcome is not in my hands.

To "let go" is not to try to change or blame another,
it is to make the most of myself.

To "let go" is not to fix, but
to support.

To "let go" is not to be in the middle arranging all the outcomes, but
to allow others to affect their own destiny.

To "let go" is not to be protective, but
to permit another to face reality.

To "let go" is not to deny, but
to accept.

To "let go" is not to nag, scold, or argue, but instead
to search out my own shortcomings and to correct them.

To "let go" is not to adjust everything to my desires, but
to take each day as it comes, and to cherish myself in it.

To "let go" is not to criticize and regulate anybody, but
to try to become what I dream I can be.

To "let go" is not to regret the past, but
to grow and live for the future.

To "let go" is to fear less and to love more.

Put a check next to the statements with which you struggle. Then write out a prayer asking God to help you walk in healthier ways in each of those areas.

_____

_____

_____

_____

_____

_____

_____

_____

_____

_____

_____

_____

_____

_____

_____

_____

COURAGEOUS COMMITMENT TO CHANGE

1. What area do you need to change or what challenge are you facing next week?

_____

_____

2. What will it cost you emotionally if you do change? What fear will you have to face?

_____

_____

3. What will it cost you if you don't change?

_____

_____

4. What is your plan to maintain your restoration regarding these changes?

_____

_____

5. Who will keep you accountable to this commitment?

Name _____ Day _____

Name _____ Day _____

Name _____ Day _____

6. What are the details of your accountability this week? What questions should they ask?

_____

_____

_____

FASTER SCALE

Adapted with permission from the *Genesis Process* by Michael Dye

PART ONE

Circle the behaviors on the FASTER Scale that you identify with in each section.

....

Restoration – (**Accepting life on God's terms, with trust, grace, mercy, vulnerability and gratitude**.) No current secrets; working to resolve problems; identifying fears and feelings; keeping commitments to meetings, prayer, family, church, people, goals, and self; being open and honest, making eye contact; increasing in relationships with God and others; true accountability.

....

Forgetting Priorities – (**Start believing the present circumstances and moving away from trusting God. Denial; flight; a change in what's important; how you spend your time, energy, and thoughts.**) Secrets; less time/energy for God, meetings, church; avoiding support and accountability people; superficial conversations; sarcasm; isolating; changes in goals; obsessed with relationships; breaking promises & commitments; neglecting family; preoccupation with material things, TV, computers, entertainment; procrastination; lying; overconfidence; bored; hiding money; image management; seeking to control situations and other people.

....

Forgetting Priorities will lead to the inclusion of:

Anxiety – (**A growing background noise of undefined fear; getting energy from emotions.**) Worry, using profanity, being fearful; being resentful; replaying old, negative thoughts; perfectionism; judging other's motives; making goals and lists that you can't complete; mind reading; fantasy, codependent, rescuing; sleep problems, trouble concentrating, seeking/creating drama; gossip; using over-the-counter medication for pain, sleep or weight control; flirting.

....

Anxiety then leads to the inclusion of:

Speeding Up – **(Trying to outrun the anxiety which is usually the first sign of depression.)** Super busy and always in a hurry (finding good reason to justify the work); workaholic; can't relax; avoiding slowing down; feeling driven; can't turn off thoughts; skipping meals; binge eating (usually at night); overspending; can't identify own feelings/needs; repetitive negative thoughts; irritable; dramatic mood swings; too much caffeine; over exercising; nervousness; difficulty being alone and/or with people; difficulty listening to others; making excuses for having to "do it all."

....

Speeding Up then leads to the inclusion of:

Ticked Off – **(Getting adrenaline high on anger and aggression.)** Procrastination causing crisis in money, work, and relationships; increased sarcasm; black and white (all or nothing) thinking; feeling alone; nobody understands; overreacting, road rage; constant resentments; pushing others away; increasing isolation; blaming; arguing; irrational thinking; can't take criticism; defensive; people avoiding you; needing to be right; digestive problems; headaches; obsessive (stuck) thoughts; can't forgive; feeling superior; using intimidation.

....

Ticked Off then leads to the inclusion of:

Exhausted – **(Loss of physical and emotional energy; coming off the adrenaline high, and the onset of depression.)** Depressed; panicked; confused; hopelessness; sleeping too much or too little; can't cope; overwhelmed; crying for "no reason"; can't think; forgetful; pessimistic; helpless; tired; numb; wanting to run; constant cravings for old coping behaviors; thinking of using sex, drugs, or alcohol; seeking old unhealthy people & places; really isolating; people angry with you; self abuse; suicidal thoughts; spontaneous crying; no goals; survival mode; not returning phone calls; missing work; irritability; no appetite.

....

Exhausted then leads to the inclusion of:

Relapse – **(Returning to the place you swore you would never go again. Coping with life on your terms. You sitting in the driver's seat instead of God.)** Giving up and giving in; out of control; lost in your addiction; lying to yourself and others; feeling you just can't manage without your coping behaviors, at least for now. The result is the reinforcement of shame, guilt and condemnation; and feelings of abandonment and being alone.

....

PART TWO

Identify the most powerful behavior in each section and write it next to the corresponding heading.

Answer the following three questions:
1. How does it affect me? How do I feel in the moment?
2. How does it affect the important people in my life?
3. Why do I do this? What is the benefit for me?

Restoration: _____
1. _____
2. _____
3. _____

Forgetting Priorities: _____
1. _____
2. _____
3. _____

Anxiety: _____
1. _____
2. _____
3. _____

Speeding Up: _____
1. _____
2. _____
3. _____

Ticked Off: _____
1. _____
2. _____
3. _____

Exhausted: _____
1. _____
2. _____
3. _____

Relapse: _____
1. _____
2. _____
3. _____

GROUP CHECK-IN
COMPLETE 24 HOURS BEFORE GROUP

1. What is the lowest level you reached on the **FASTER Scale** this week?

_____

2. What was the **Double Bind** you were dealing with?

_____

_____

_____

_____

3. Where are you on your **Courageous Commitment to Change** from our last meeting?

_____

4. What information from your Betrayal & Beyond lesson was most applicable to your situation this week? What information had the most impact emotionally?

_____

_____

_____

5. What have you done to improve your relationship with your husband or other significant relationships this week?

_____

_____

_____

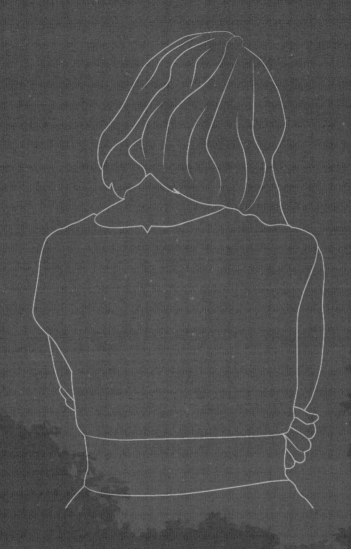

Chapter Nine

RESTORING HEALTH AND CLOSENESS

Lesson One
THE ADDICT'S PERSPECTIVE

Thought for the week: *You are beginning the final phase of your heroine's journey. Your quest has led you through challenges from which you have emerged stronger. As you prepare for this stage, take time to listen to God speaking words of encouragement over you.*

List five things you are thankful for this week.

1. _____
2. _____
3. _____
4. _____
5. _____

Write down the personal/prophetic promises God has shown you so far with the Scripture He has given you.

1. _____
2. _____
3. _____
4. _____
5. _____

If your small group released balloons (or will release them this week) in response to the poem, *Letting Go*, summarize your feelings and thoughts about that experience.

_____

_____

_____

Summarize your response to the information the addicts shared from the panel in Lesson one of your *Workbook* and explain whose testimony you could relate to the most.

_____

_____

_____

How would you define your marriage at this point in your journey?

_____

_____

_____

Write out a prayer for your marriage and yourself concerning where you are in your journey.

_____

_____

_____

_____

_____

_____

Listen to God encouraging you in the battle. Write down what you sense He is saying.

_____

_____

_____

_____

Thank God for understanding your pain and for all He is doing to help you in this difficult time. Thank Him for the things you know He will do.

_____

_____

_____

_____

Spend time listening to God share how precious you are. Write what He says to you and your response to the prayer the men prayed over the women in this lesson.

_____

_____

_____

_____

If your marriage has already ended, write out your feelings about what Teri expressed in her testimony at the end of this lesson.

_____

_____

_____

_____

How can the women in your group be praying for you in light of your marriage ending?

_____

_____

_____

_____

If your marriage is over, the next exercise may not apply unless you share children together. Instead of the following exercise, write a letter to God asking Him to help your ex-husband become the father your children need him to be.

If you are still married, and especially if your spouse is a part of a Pure Desire men's group, it is important that you take the next step towards forgiveness. That next step is writing him a letter entitled, "The Man I See You Becoming." We know that, at this point, he has not completed his healing journey, but it is still important for you to acknowledge any changes you see in him, and it is very important for him to hear that you recognize the new things God is doing in him. If need be, refer back to your other letter: Chapter 7, Lesson 1, "The Man I Thought I Married" and Chapter 7, Lesson 3, "The Man I Realize I Married." This may be a letter in process, but it is important that you recognize even some baby steps your husband may be taking toward permanent change.

To The Man I See You Becoming:

_____

_____

_____

_____

_____

_____

_____

COURAGEOUS COMMITMENT TO CHANGE

1. What area do you need to change or what challenge are you facing next week?

_____

_____

2. What will it cost you emotionally if you do change? What fear will you have to face?

_____

_____

3. What will it cost you if you don't change?

_____

_____

4. What is your plan to maintain your restoration regarding these changes?

_____

_____

5. Who will keep you accountable to this commitment?

Name _____   Day _____

Name _____   Day _____

Name _____   Day _____

6. What are the details of your accountability this week? What questions should they ask?

_____

_____

_____

FASTER SCALE

Adapted with permission from the *Genesis Process* by Michael Dye

PART ONE

Circle the behaviors on the FASTER Scale that you identify with in each section.

....

Restoration – (**Accepting life on God's terms, with trust, grace, mercy, vulnerability and gratitude**.) No current secrets; working to resolve problems; identifying fears and feelings; keeping commitments to meetings, prayer, family, church, people, goals, and self; being open and honest, making eye contact; increasing in relationships with God and others; true accountability.

....

Forgetting Priorities – (**Start believing the present circumstances and moving away from trusting God. Denial; flight; a change in what's important; how you spend your time, energy, and thoughts.**) Secrets; less time/energy for God, meetings, church; avoiding support and accountability people; superficial conversations; sarcasm; isolating; changes in goals; obsessed with relationships; breaking promises & commitments; neglecting family; preoccupation with material things, TV, computers, entertainment; procrastination; lying; overconfidence; bored; hiding money; image management; seeking to control situations and other people.

....

Forgetting Priorities will lead to the inclusion of:

Anxiety – (**A growing background noise of undefined fear; getting energy from emotions.**) Worry, using profanity, being fearful; being resentful; replaying old, negative thoughts; perfectionism; judging other's motives; making goals and lists that you can't complete; mind reading; fantasy, codependent, rescuing; sleep problems, trouble concentrating, seeking/creating drama; gossip; using over-the-counter medication for pain, sleep or weight control; flirting.

....

Anxiety then leads to the inclusion of:

Speeding Up – **(Trying to outrun the anxiety which is usually the first sign of depression.)** Super busy and always in a hurry (finding good reason to justify the work); workaholic; can't relax; avoiding slowing down; feeling driven; can't turn off thoughts; skipping meals; binge eating (usually at night); overspending; can't identify own feelings/needs; repetitive negative thoughts; irritable; dramatic mood swings; too much caffeine; over exercising; nervousness; difficulty being alone and/or with people; difficulty listening to others; making excuses for having to "do it all."

....

Speeding Up then leads to the inclusion of:

Ticked Off – **(Getting adrenaline high on anger and aggression.)** Procrastination causing crisis in money, work, and relationships; increased sarcasm; black and white (all or nothing) thinking; feeling alone; nobody understands; overreacting, road rage; constant resentments; pushing others away; increasing isolation; blaming; arguing; irrational thinking; can't take criticism; defensive; people avoiding you; needing to be right; digestive problems; headaches; obsessive (stuck) thoughts; can't forgive; feeling superior; using intimidation.

....

Ticked Off then leads to the inclusion of:

Exhausted – **(Loss of physical and emotional energy; coming off the adrenaline high, and the onset of depression.)** Depressed; panicked; confused; hopelessness; sleeping too much or too little; can't cope; overwhelmed; crying for "no reason"; can't think; forgetful; pessimistic; helpless; tired; numb; wanting to run; constant cravings for old coping behaviors; thinking of using sex, drugs, or alcohol; seeking old unhealthy people & places; really isolating; people angry with you; self abuse; suicidal thoughts; spontaneous crying; no goals; survival mode; not returning phone calls; missing work; irritability; no appetite.

....

Exhausted then leads to the inclusion of:

Relapse – **(Returning to the place you swore you would never go again. Coping with life on your terms. You sitting in the driver's seat instead of God.)** Giving up and giving in; out of control; lost in your addiction; lying to yourself and others; feeling you just can't manage without your coping behaviors, at least for now. The result is the reinforcement of shame, guilt and condemnation; and feelings of abandonment and being alone.

....

PART TWO

Identify the most powerful behavior in each section and write it next to the corresponding heading.

Answer the following three questions:
1. How does it affect me? How do I feel in the moment?
2. How does it affect the important people in my life?
3. Why do I do this? What is the benefit for me?

Restoration: _____
1. _____
2. _____
3. _____

Forgetting Priorities: _____
1. _____
2. _____
3. _____

Anxiety: _____
1. _____
2. _____
3. _____

Speeding Up: _____
1. _____
2. _____
3. _____

Ticked Off: _____
1. _____
2. _____
3. _____

Exhausted: _____
1. _____
2. _____
3. _____

Relapse: _____
1. _____
2. _____
3. _____

GROUP CHECK-IN
COMPLETE 24 HOURS BEFORE GROUP

1. What is the lowest level you reached on the **FASTER Scale** this week?

_____

2. What was the **Double Bind** you were dealing with?

_____

_____

_____

_____

3. Where are you on your **Courageous Commitment to Change** from our last meeting?

_____

4. What information from your Betrayal & Beyond lesson was most applicable to your situation this week? What information had the most impact emotionally?

_____

_____

_____

5. What have you done to improve your relationship with your husband or other significant relationships this week?

_____

_____

_____

📄 Lesson Two

THE WIFE'S PERSPECTIVE: SHOULD I STAY OR SHOULD I LEAVE?

Thought for the week: As you continue to travel this journey, you will find that it is about balance. While it is important to be kind, it is also important that you do not let others abuse you. You have learned many tools along this journey that will help you learn to trust, while not allowing yourself to be deceived.

List five things you are thankful for this week.

1. _____

2. _____

3. _____

4. _____

5. _____

Write down the personal/prophetic promises God has shown you so far with the Scripture He has given you.

1. _____

2. _____

3. _____

4. _____

5. _____

After listing areas Trina's husband might not be safe in your *Workbook*, list the areas where your husband may seem unsafe.

_____

_____

_____

_____

Write out a prayer for your spouse in light of these unsafe areas.

Dear Lord,

_____

_____

_____

_____

_____

_____

Where do you struggle in becoming a safe person? Write a prayer asking God to help you become a safe person.

Dear Lord,

_____

_____

_____

_____

_____

_____

For additional insight into what healthy and safe relationship looks like, watch Brene Brown's[5] presentation on trust and summarize what you learned in each of the following categories: www.supersoul.tv/supersoul-sessions/the-anatomy-of-trust/

BRAVING – THE ANATOMY OF TRUST

B – Boundaries. You respect my boundaries.

R – Reliability. You do what you say you'll do.

A – Accountability. You own your mistakes, apologize, and make amends.

V – Vault. You don't share information or experiences that are not yours to share.

I – Integrity. You choose courage over comfort.

N – Non-judgment. I can ask for what I need, and you can ask for what you need. We can talk about how we feel without judgment.

G – Generosity. You extend the most generous interpretation possible to the intentions, words and actions of others.

....

5. Brene Brown, *Rising Strong* (New York: Random House, 2015).

COURAGEOUS COMMITMENT TO CHANGE

1. What area do you need to change or what challenge are you facing next week?

_____

_____

2. What will it cost you emotionally if you do change? What fear will you have to face?

_____

_____

3. What will it cost you if you don't change?

_____

_____

4. What is your plan to maintain your restoration regarding these changes?

_____

_____

5. Who will keep you accountable to this commitment?

Name _____   Day _____

Name _____   Day _____

Name _____   Day _____

6. What are the details of your accountability this week? What questions should they ask?

_____

_____

_____

FASTER SCALE

Adapted with permission from the *Genesis Process* by Michael Dye

PART ONE

Circle the behaviors on the FASTER Scale that you identify with in each section.

....

Restoration – **(Accepting life on God's terms, with trust, grace, mercy, vulnerability and gratitude.)** No current secrets; working to resolve problems; identifying fears and feelings; keeping commitments to meetings, prayer, family, church, people, goals, and self; being open and honest, making eye contact; increasing in relationships with God and others; true accountability.

....

Forgetting Priorities – **(Start believing the present circumstances and moving away from trusting God. Denial; flight; a change in what's important; how you spend your time, energy, and thoughts.)** Secrets; less time/energy for God, meetings, church; avoiding support and accountability people; superficial conversations; sarcasm; isolating; changes in goals; obsessed with relationships; breaking promises & commitments; neglecting family; preoccupation with material things, TV, computers, entertainment; procrastination; lying; overconfidence; bored; hiding money; image management; seeking to control situations and other people.

....

Forgetting Priorities will lead to the inclusion of:

Anxiety – **(A growing background noise of undefined fear; getting energy from emotions.)** Worry, using profanity, being fearful; being resentful; replaying old, negative thoughts; perfectionism; judging other's motives; making goals and lists that you can't complete; mind reading; fantasy, codependent, rescuing; sleep problems, trouble concentrating, seeking/creating drama; gossip; using over-the-counter medication for pain, sleep or weight control; flirting.

....

Anxiety then leads to the inclusion of:

Speeding Up – **(Trying to outrun the anxiety which is usually the first sign of depression.)** Super busy and always in a hurry (finding good reason to justify the work); workaholic; can't relax; avoiding slowing down; feeling driven; can't turn off thoughts; skipping meals; binge eating (usually at night); overspending; can't identify own feelings/needs; repetitive negative thoughts; irritable; dramatic mood swings; too much caffeine; over exercising; nervousness; difficulty being alone and/or with people; difficulty listening to others; making excuses for having to "do it all."

....

Speeding Up then leads to the inclusion of:

Ticked Off – **(Getting adrenaline high on anger and aggression.)** Procrastination causing crisis in money, work, and relationships; increased sarcasm; black and white (all or nothing) thinking; feeling alone; nobody understands; overreacting, road rage; constant resentments; pushing others away; increasing isolation; blaming; arguing; irrational thinking; can't take criticism; defensive; people avoiding you; needing to be right; digestive problems; headaches; obsessive (stuck) thoughts; can't forgive; feeling superior; using intimidation.

....

Ticked Off then leads to the inclusion of:

Exhausted – **(Loss of physical and emotional energy; coming off the adrenaline high, and the onset of depression.)** Depressed; panicked; confused; hopelessness; sleeping too much or too little; can't cope; overwhelmed; crying for "no reason"; can't think; forgetful; pessimistic; helpless; tired; numb; wanting to run; constant cravings for old coping behaviors; thinking of using sex, drugs, or alcohol; seeking old unhealthy people & places; really isolating; people angry with you; self abuse; suicidal thoughts; spontaneous crying; no goals; survival mode; not returning phone calls; missing work; irritability; no appetite.

....

Exhausted then leads to the inclusion of:

Relapse – **(Returning to the place you swore you would never go again. Coping with life on your terms. You sitting in the driver's seat instead of God.)** Giving up and giving in; out of control; lost in your addiction; lying to yourself and others; feeling you just can't manage without your coping behaviors, at least for now. The result is the reinforcement of shame, guilt and condemnation; and feelings of abandonment and being alone.

....

PART TWO

Identify the most powerful behavior in each section and write it next to the corresponding heading.

Answer the following three questions:

    1. How does it affect me? How do I feel in the moment?

    2. How does it affect the important people in my life?

    3. Why do I do this? What is the benefit for me?

Restoration: _____

1. _____

2. _____

3. _____

Forgetting Priorities: _____

1. _____

2. _____

3. _____

Anxiety: _____

1. _____

2. _____

3. _____

Speeding Up: _____

1. _____

2. _____

3. _____

Ticked Off: _____

1. _____

2. _____

3. _____

Exhausted: _____

1. _____

2. _____

3. _____

Relapse: _____

1. _____

2. _____

3. _____

GROUP CHECK-IN
COMPLETE 24 HOURS BEFORE GROUP

1. What is the lowest level you reached on the **FASTER Scale** this week?

_____

2. What was the **Double Bind** you were dealing with?

_____

_____

_____

_____

3. Where are you on your **Courageous Commitment to Change** from our last meeting?

_____

4. What information from your Betrayal & Beyond lesson was most applicable to your situation this week? What information had the most impact emotionally?

_____

_____

_____

5. What have you done to improve your relationship with your husband or other significant relationships this week?

_____

_____

_____

⬘ *Lesson Three*

A HEALTHY MARRIAGE PERSPECTIVE ON INTIMACY AND SEX

Thought for the week: *In her heart, a heroine is a princess who wants to be pursued by her prince. She wants her heart to be safe in his hands, but because of the trials she has experienced, she may be afraid to risk again. The heroine is facing her most challenging Double Bind.*

List five things you are thankful for this week.

1. _____
2. _____
3. _____
4. _____
5. _____

Write down the personal/prophetic promises God has shown you so far with the Scripture He has given you.

1. _____
2. _____
3. _____
4. _____
5. _____

With all you have gone through in this healing process, share on a scale of 1-10 how ready you are to pursue intimacy. This may be predicated on him working hard in a Pure Desire men's group.

Not so willing   Very willing

1	2	3	4	5	6	7	8	9	10

Journal your fears of taking this next step.

_____

_____

_____

_____

_____

_____

_____

_____

_____

_____

_____

_____

_____

_____

At this stage in your healing, in what ways could he pursue you? Come up with your own ideas or use some from the following list. Plan to update your list periodically, as more ideas come to mind.

The ideas listed are non-sexual in nature to allow your spouse to begin to court you and put you first in the relationship. If he has been through most of the Seven Pillars of Freedom group for men, he should be ready to take this step.

SUGGESTIONS FOR PURSUING YOUR WIFE

1. Surprise her! She loves all types of surprises, anything from a special note or card left out, to flowers, to a specially planned date night (remember it's the thought that counts).

2. Give her a gift. It can be big or small (e.g. something you made at work, a treat from the store, a book, a movie, a gift card to somewhere she likes, or jewelry). Anything that says you were thinking of her makes a good gift.

3. Plan quality time with her and tell her in advance so she can look forward to her time with you. Letting her know that you want to spend time with her makes her feel special.

4. Plan a date night and don't ask her what she wants to do, but surprise her instead. Think of things that she would like to do or things you like doing together. Your thoughtful planning makes her feel like she's worth your time.

5. Tell her how you feel about her (What do you love about her? What do you appreciate about her?). Compliment her (What physical qualities do you like about her? What inner qualities do you like about her?). You can never compliment her too much. Though make sure your comment is genuine, because she can tell when you aren't being genuine. This can be done through a verbal comment, text, card, or phone call, any way you like to express yourself.

6. Tell her often that you love her or that you miss her. She can never hear these things too much.

7. Text her when you are thinking about her. She loves to hear that she's on your mind. She desires to be the only woman in your heart and loves to hear when you're thinking of her.

8. She loves to be physically touched (I am not talking about sexual touch). Hug her. Kiss her. Wrap your arm around her. Rub her arm or her back. She wants to know that she's your woman and you're not afraid to tell others about her.

9. Initiate lovemaking. When you initiate, it makes her feel like you want to be with her. You can initiate by leaving a rose on the pillow, or planning and asking her in advance.

DATE NIGHT IDEAS

- Go bowling, go mini golfing, play tennis, go roller skating, play pool, plan dinner out, plan a game night, go horseback riding, go hiking, attend a concert, or go to a drive-in theatre.

- Plan and pack a picnic lunch for the park or beach.

- Go for a walk or bike ride (maybe even get ice cream along the way).

- Watch a movie (especially one your wife would like to see…you'll get real brownie points if it's a chick flick).

- Find somewhere to have a campfire, stargaze, or chase a storm.

- How about a spa date? Go get pedicures together.

- Look up events in your town to go to (e.g. exhibits, museums, plays, jazz festival).

WAYS YOUR SPOUSE CAN PURSUE YOU

_____

_____

_____

_____

_____

DATE NIGHT IDEAS

_____

_____

_____

_____

Who will hold you accountable to share these with your spouse this week?

_____

If you struggle sharing these with your spouse, write about your struggle. If need be, do a Double Bind exercise. (If I don't share them, I will not experience intimacy in my marriage or find my voice. If I risk and share these, I will have to face the fear of him laughing and/or rejecting what I stated I need.)

_____

_____

_____

_____

What are some things you can accept about your spouse? (Such as: His healing may take longer than you thought, his trauma has had an impact on his behavior, his addictive behaviors have led to difficult circumstances. He also may be slow in gaining empathy skills because most addicts come from rigid, disengaged homes with little or no experience with attachment and empathy). **Pray and journal about what you can accept at this point.**

_____

_____

_____

_____

After reading the section of what you might need for safety to resume a sexual relationship, write out your needs regarding safety, so that you can feel truly honest in your sexual union with your husband.

_____

_____

_____

_____

_____

At the end of your *Workbook* lesson for this week, you were challenged to pray and ask God to open your heart to be healed in this extremely important area of your life.

Dear God,

_____

_____

_____

_____

_____

_____

_____

_____

_____

Write out one thing you would like your spouse to understand about your sexual feelings. After writing it out, read it to him or give it to him to read. (You may want to look at the Developing Intimacy Exercise available in your *Betrayal & Beyond Workbook* appendix, page 298.)

_____

_____

_____

_____

_____

_____

_____

_____

_____

COURAGEOUS COMMITMENT TO CHANGE

1. What area do you need to change or what challenge are you facing next week?

_____

_____

2. What will it cost you emotionally if you do change? What fear will you have to face?

_____

_____

3. What will it cost you if you don't change?

_____

_____

4. What is your plan to maintain your restoration regarding these changes?

_____

_____

5. Who will keep you accountable to this commitment?

Name _____   Day _____

Name _____   Day _____

Name _____   Day _____

6. What are the details of your accountability this week? What questions should they ask?

_____

_____

_____

FASTER SCALE

Adapted with permission from the *Genesis Process* by Michael Dye

PART ONE

Circle the behaviors on the FASTER Scale that you identify with in each section.

....

Restoration – (**Accepting life on God's terms, with trust, grace, mercy, vulnerability and gratitude**.) No current secrets; working to resolve problems; identifying fears and feelings; keeping commitments to meetings, prayer, family, church, people, goals, and self; being open and honest, making eye contact; increasing in relationships with God and others; true accountability.

....

Forgetting Priorities – (**Start believing the present circumstances and moving away from trusting God. Denial; flight; a change in what's important; how you spend your time, energy, and thoughts.**) Secrets; less time/energy for God, meetings, church; avoiding support and accountability people; superficial conversations; sarcasm; isolating; changes in goals; obsessed with relationships; breaking promises & commitments; neglecting family; preoccupation with material things, TV, computers, entertainment; procrastination; lying; overconfidence; bored; hiding money; image management; seeking to control situations and other people.

....

Forgetting Priorities will lead to the inclusion of:

Anxiety – (**A growing background noise of undefined fear; getting energy from emotions.**) Worry, using profanity, being fearful; being resentful; replaying old, negative thoughts; perfectionism; judging other's motives; making goals and lists that you can't complete; mind reading; fantasy, codependent, rescuing; sleep problems, trouble concentrating, seeking/creating drama; gossip; using over-the-counter medication for pain, sleep or weight control; flirting.

....

253

Anxiety then leads to the inclusion of:

Speeding Up – **(Trying to outrun the anxiety which is usually the first sign of depression.)** Super busy and always in a hurry (finding good reason to justify the work); workaholic; can't relax; avoiding slowing down; feeling driven; can't turn off thoughts; skipping meals; binge eating (usually at night); overspending; can't identify own feelings/needs; repetitive negative thoughts; irritable; dramatic mood swings; too much caffeine; over exercising; nervousness; difficulty being alone and/or with people; difficulty listening to others; making excuses for having to "do it all."

....

Speeding Up then leads to the inclusion of:

Ticked Off – **(Getting adrenaline high on anger and aggression.)** Procrastination causing crisis in money, work, and relationships; increased sarcasm; black and white (all or nothing) thinking; feeling alone; nobody understands; overreacting, road rage; constant resentments; pushing others away; increasing isolation; blaming; arguing; irrational thinking; can't take criticism; defensive; people avoiding you; needing to be right; digestive problems; headaches; obsessive (stuck) thoughts; can't forgive; feeling superior; using intimidation.

....

Ticked Off then leads to the inclusion of:

Exhausted – **(Loss of physical and emotional energy; coming off the adrenaline high, and the onset of depression.)** Depressed; panicked; confused; hopelessness; sleeping too much or too little; can't cope; overwhelmed; crying for "no reason"; can't think; forgetful; pessimistic; helpless; tired; numb; wanting to run; constant cravings for old coping behaviors; thinking of using sex, drugs, or alcohol; seeking old unhealthy people & places; really isolating; people angry with you; self abuse; suicidal thoughts; spontaneous crying; no goals; survival mode; not returning phone calls; missing work; irritability; no appetite.

....

Exhausted then leads to the inclusion of:

Relapse – **(Returning to the place you swore you would never go again. Coping with life on your terms. You sitting in the driver's seat instead of God.)** Giving up and giving in; out of control; lost in your addiction; lying to yourself and others; feeling you just can't manage without your coping behaviors, at least for now. The result is the reinforcement of shame, guilt and condemnation; and feelings of abandonment and being alone.

....

PART TWO

Identify the most powerful behavior in each section and write it next to the corresponding heading.

Answer the following three questions:
1. How does it affect me? How do I feel in the moment?
2. How does it affect the important people in my life?
3. Why do I do this? What is the benefit for me?

Restoration: _____
1. _____
2. _____
3. _____

Forgetting Priorities: _____
1. _____
2. _____
3. _____

Anxiety: _____
1. _____
2. _____
3. _____

Speeding Up: _____
1. _____
2. _____
3. _____

Ticked Off: _____
1. _____
2. _____
3. _____

Exhausted: _____
1. _____
2. _____
3. _____

Relapse: _____
1. _____
2. _____
3. _____

GROUP CHECK-IN
COMPLETE 24 HOURS BEFORE GROUP

1. What is the lowest level you reached on the **FASTER Scale** this week?

_____

2. What was the **Double Bind** you were dealing with?

_____

_____

_____

_____

3. Where are you on your **Courageous Commitment to Change** from our last meeting?

_____

4. What information from your Betrayal & Beyond lesson was most applicable to your situation this week? What information had the most impact emotionally?

_____

_____

_____

5. What have you done to improve your relationship with your husband or other significant relationships this week?

_____

_____

_____

ⓘ 𝓛𝑒𝓈𝓈𝑜𝓃 𝓕𝑜𝓊𝓇

A PERSPECTIVE FOR THE FUTURE

Thought for the week: *Your Journey is not over yet. You may need one last push from your fellow heroines to face your final challenge. The result of this battle will have far-reaching impact, as you courageously determine the outcome of your journey.*

List five things you are thankful for this week.

1. _____
2. _____
3. _____
4. _____
5. _____

Write down the personal/prophetic promises God has shown you so far with the Scripture He has given you.

1. _____
2. _____
3. _____
4. _____
5. _____

REVIEW THESE STATEMENTS FROM YOUR WORKBOOK

Our weapons against the enemy:

- Deciding to allow God's Word to reign in your life rather than letting your feelings rule your life.

- Obeying God despite the difficulties you are going through.

- Doing what is right despite the costs.

- Facing your selfish desires and behavior, then choosing not be controlled by shame and fear, but to accept God's grace instead.

Which of those listed above are most difficult for you to walk in? Explain.

_____

_____

_____

_____

_____

_____

How might your personal/prophetic promises help you in this battle?

_____

_____

_____

_____

_____

_____

As you prepare to work on your Three Circles, read chapters seven through ten in Exodus. Notice a fascinating phenomenon: Initially, the plagues that God brought upon the land hit both the Egyptians and Israelites. But by the fourth plague, things changed. God declared that He would make a distinction between His people and the Egyptians. None of the remaining plagues hit the camp of the Israelites.

Initially the plagues hit the just and the unjust. As followers of Christ, we can't escape difficulties in this life and we definitely can't medicate them away. Although our faith doesn't insulate us from problems, there is a "corporate anointing." What do these Scriptures say about a "corporate anointing?"

- Matthew 18:19-20
- Acts 2:1-4
- Acts 4:23-31

A Holy Spirit anointing enables you to walk differently in this world, especially as you chose to walk with other trusted women.

As this group ends, what is your plan to continue walking in a "corporate anointing?"

_____

_____

_____

_____

_____

_____

_____

_____

_____

_____

_____

A Couple's Safety Plan, which can be found in the *Betrayal & Beyond Workbook* appendix, page 300, gives you ideas as to how, as a couple, you can continue to build trust and grow in intimacy in your relationship.

Ask your husband if he'd like to make a Couple's Safety Plan together and list some of the suggestion you'd like to make for that safety plan.

1. _____

2. _____

3. _____

4. _____

5. _____

6. _____

In the *Workbook*, we looked at the hidden treasures God placed in people from the Bible. In light of this, what has God hidden inside of you?

> *But we have this treasure in earthen vessels,*
> *that the excellence of the power may be of God and not of us.*
> 2 CORINTHIANS 4:7 (NKJV)

_____

_____

_____

What gifts would you like to leave for others that could be included in your "dash?"

_____

_____

_____

_____

Using the prayer suggestions in the *Workbook*, personalize and write out your own prayer.

Dear Lord,

_____

_____

_____

_____

_____

_____

_____

_____

_____

_____

_____

_____

Signed: _____

CONGRATULATIONS!

You have reached the final stage of your *heroine's journey* and have emerged from your battle a changed woman. You have learned much, faced many challenges, and grown as a person. You have experienced the importance of walking with other, trusted women as you battle against the enemy to earn your rewards: Growing intimacy in relationships, rediscovering your dreams, and determining your legacy. And, now, you may look forward to sharing that victory with others, as you are now equipped to mentor and bring fresh hope to women who are just beginning their own journey.

As you begin your new, upgraded *status quo*, celebrate the *heroine* you have become.